Modern Imperialism, Monopoly Finance Capital, and Marx's law of value

Modern Imperialism, Monopoly Finance Capital, and Marx's Law of Value

SAMIR AMIN

MONTHLY REVIEW PRESS

New York

Copyright © 2018 by Samir Amin
All Rights Reserved

Library of Congress Cataloging-in-Publication Data
available from the publisher.

ISBN (paper): 978-1-58367-655-4
ISBN (cloth): 978-1-58367-656-1

MONTHLY REVIEW PRESS
NEW YORK

www.monthlyreview.org

5 4 3 2 1

Contents

PART ONE

The Law of Worldwide Value

Introduction to the English Edition

Marx is not a philosopher, a historian, an economist, a political scientist, or a sociologist. He is not even a scholar of the first rank in any of those disciplines. Nor even a talented professor who prepared a good multidisciplinary dish cooked with all these ingredients. Marx's place is quite outside all that. Marx is the beginning of the radical critique of modern times, starting with the critique of the real world. This radical critique of capitalism demands and allows discovery of the basis of market alienation and, inseparable from it, the exploitation of labor. *The foundational status of the concept of value derives from this radical critique.* It alone allows a grasp of the objective laws that govern the reproduction of the system, underlying those surface movements perceptible through direct observation of reality. Marx links to this critique of the real world the critique of discourses about that reality: those of philosophy, economics, sociology, history, and political science. This radical critique uncovers their true nature which, in the last analysis, is always an apologetic one, legitimizing the practices of capital's dominating power.

To be a "Marxist" is to continue the work that Marx merely began, even though that beginning was of an unequaled power. It is not to stop at Marx, but to start from him. For Marx is not a prophet whose conclusions, drawn from a critique of both reality and how it has been read, are all necessarily "correct" or "final." His opus is not a closed theory. Marx is *boundless*, because the radical critique that he initiated is itself boundless, always incomplete, and must always be the object of its own critique ("Marxism as formulated at a particular moment has to undergo a Marxist critique"), must unceasingly enrich itself through radical critique, treating whatever novelties the real system produces as newly opened fields of knowledge.

The subtitle of *Capital*—"A Critique of Political Economy"— does not mean a critique of a "bad" (Ricardian) political economy, with a view to replacing it with a "good" (Marxian) one. It is rather a critique of so-called economic science, an exposure of its true nature (as what the bourgeoisie has to say about its own practice); and so of its epistemological status, an exposure of its limitations, and an invitation to realize that this alleged science, claimed to be independent of historical materialism, cannot possess such independence. Political economy is the outward form assumed by historical materialism (the class struggle) under capitalism. On the logical plane historical materialism is prior to economics, but class struggle under capitalism does not take place in a vacuum: it operates on an economic basis, and shapes laws that appear economic in character.

I shall study this articulation first as it is presented in *Capital* itself, that is, in the theory of the capitalist mode of production, and then in the reality of the capitalist system of our own day—in imperialism.

My thesis is: (a) that historical materialism constitutes the essence of Marxism; and therefore (b) that the epistemological status of the economic laws of capitalism is such that they are subordinate to the laws of historical materialism; (c) that under the capitalist mode of production economic laws possess a theoretical status different from that which they possess under precapitalist modes; and even (d) that, strictly speaking, economic laws are to be found only under the capitalist mode; (e) that the economic laws of capitalism do indeed exist objectively; and, finally, (f) that these laws are governed, in the last analysis, by the law of value.

Thus, in my view, the class struggle under capitalism in general, and in the imperialist world system in particular, operates on a definite economic basis and, in its turn, changes that basis.

My readings in Marx certainly brought considerable intellectual fulfillment and convinced me of the power of his thought. Still, I was left unsatisfied. For I was asking a central question, that of the "underdevelopment" of contemporary Asian and African societies, and I found no answer in Marx. Far from "abandoning" Marx and counting him "outdated," I simply came to the conclusion that his opus had remained incomplete. Marx had not finished the opus that he had set out to complete, and that included not integrating the "global dimension" of capitalism into his analysis. So I have tried to do so. The central axis of the conclusions reached by my efforts is defined by the formulation of a "law of globalized value," coherent, on the one hand, with the bases of the law of value proper to capitalism as discovered by Marx and, on the other, with the realities of unequal globalized development.

My major contribution concerns the *passage from the law of value to the law of globalized value,* based on the hierarchical structuring—itself globalized—of the prices of labor-power around its value. Linked to the management practices governing access to natural resources, this globalization of value constitutes the basis for *imperialist rent.* This, I claim, orders the unfolding of really existing capitalism/imperialism's contradictions and of the conflicts linked to them, so that classes and nations are imbricated, in their struggles and clashes, in all the complex articulation, specific and concrete, of those contradictions. I claim that our reading of the twentieth and twenty-first centuries can be nothing other than that of the emergence—or of the "reawakening"—of peoples and nations peripheric to the globalized capitalist/imperialist system.

In order to carry out my exposition, I have chosen to take up
again my book *The Law of Value and Historical Materialism* in a
new, revised and expanded, edition. In the extensive borrowings
that I have made from this old (1978) book I have conserved its
essential argument. The new paragraphs draw the reader's attention to the challenging questions arising from that retained exposition. If them I have tried to present synthetic explanations
which—in themselves adequate—do not preclude coming back
to deeper readings.

My theoretical analysis of the really existent globalized capitalist system starts from the law of value formulated by Marx in
Volume I of *Capital*. There is no other possible point of depar-
ture, because without the concept of value there is no meaning to
that of the accumulation of capital—and so we cannot skip over
this detour through value in favor of a direct grasp of reality—
which is implied by a positivist/empiricist methodology, as
revealed through observed prices.

The analysis that I am putting forward thus looks next at the
three stages in the transformation of value: (1) into "prices of production"; (2) into "market prices" (oligopolistic prices, in contemporary capitalism); and (3) into "globalized prices" (in the
globalized imperialist system).

The first of these transformations, taken up in the first chapters of Volume III of *Capital*, is indispensable to grasping the
meaning of the market alienation that governs economic and
social life under capitalism and to giving to the laws ruling its systemic reproduction their true stature.

The second of these transformations, that of prices of production into "market prices," had been partially treated by Marx, also
in Volume III of *Capital*, in the instance, among others, when he
came to consider the distribution of surplus-value in regard to
agrarian landownership. We have next to consider the deforma-
tions of the price system linked to the emergence of oligopo-
lies/monopolies and above all to take fully into account the gigan-

tic transformation of the system of expanded equilibrium resulting, after the First, but above all after the Second World War, from the accelerated expansion of a third department—of absorption of surplus surplus-value. Baran and Sweezy, with the concept of surplus that they put forward, replied to the challenge and unhesitatingly extended and enriched Marxian theory. I claim that those Marxists who still refuse to recognize the central importance of Baran and Sweezy's contribution lack the means to put forth an effective critique of contemporary capitalism. Their "Marxism" thus remains confined to exegeses of Marx's texts.

The central object of my reflections has been the third transformation, which allows us to go from the law of value, taken at its highest level of abstraction (the capitalist mode of production), to what I have called the law of globalized value, which is operative on the scale of the really extant polarizing system of capitalism/imperialism. It is only this transformation that allows us to take the measure of the imperialist rent which is at the origin of the polarization deepened and reproduced by the globalized unfolding of capitalism.

It is impossible to "understand the world" by a realistic analysis of really existing capitalism outside the framework traced by the treatment of these transformations of value. Equally, a strategy aiming to "change the world" can be based only on these foundations. As against this, the positivist/empiricist method of vulgar economics allows us neither to "understand the world" and to grasp the nature of the challenges confronting workers and peoples, nor, a fortiori, to "change" it. Furthermore, that vulgar economics does not seek to go beyond capitalism, which it sees as the "end of history." It seeks only to legitimize the basic principles of capitalism and to show how to manage it.

I believe that this new edition, drawn broadly from *The Law of Value and Historical Materialism*, comes at the right moment. This is because the current crisis revolves altogether around different possible developments of the social and international relationships that govern the form of the law of value, under the combined effects of popular struggles in the central and peripheral societies of contemporary capitalism and of struggles between dominant imperialist societies and those of the dominated periphery—struggles that call into question the continued dominance of what I call "the later capitalism of the generalized, financialized, and globalized oligopolies."

CHAPTER ONE

The Fundamental Status
of the Law of Value

After devoting Volume I of *Capital* to the foundations of the law of value, Marx concerns himself in Volume II with what might seem to be a purely "economic" argument. He tries, in fact, to show that accumulation can take place in a "pure" capitalist system, and to determine the technical conditions for dynamic equilibrium.

In Marx's illustrative examples, the system is characterized by a certain number of magnitudes and proportions, all of which belong strictly to the economic field. These magnitudes and proportions are: (a) the proportions in which labor-power and means of production are distributed between the two departments that define the main basis of the social division of labor, making possible the *simultaneous* production of means of production and of consumer goods; (b) the proportions that characterize, for each department, the degree of intensity in the use of means of production by direct labor; this intensity measures the level of development of the productive forces; (c) the evolution from one phase to another of these latter proportions, measuring the pace and direction of the progress of the productive forces; and (d) the rate of exploitation of labor (the rate of surplus-value).

Marx offers a series of examples in which the magnitudes are all given in value terms, and he is right to do so. But what he deduces from these examples—namely the economic conditions for expanded reproduction—could, to some extent, be deduced in the same way from a model constructed directly in terms of prices of production, in which profit is shown in proportion to capital employed and not to labor exploited. Within this precise and limited context, the two arguments, both of them "economic," are equivalent to each other.

There is nothing, then, to prevent one from expressing directly—in terms either of value or of price—the general economic conditions for expanded reproduction by formulating a system of linear equations in which the various variable magnitudes allowed to each department, defined correctly in relation to the parameters of sectoral distribution and of evolution from one phase to the next, are related to each other by the equality in value from one phase to the next in the respective supply of and demand for consumer goods and means of production.

I have done this—in value terms, defining, with the Greek letters lambda (λ) and gamma (γ), two parameters for measuring the progress of the productive forces in each department and from one phase to the next, and then characterizing this progress by the increase in the physical quantity of use-values produced with a decreasing quantity of labor. I therefore set out a model of expanded reproduction (with progress in the productive forces) which is defined simply as follows:

PHASE 1:

Department I: Production of means of production

$$1e + ah = pe$$

(meaning a hours of direct labor, using 1 unit of equipment and raw material, produce p units of equipment).

Department II: Production of consumer goods

$$1e + bh = qc$$

(meaning: b hours of direct labor, using 1 unit of equipment and raw material, produce q units of consumer goods).

PHASE 2:

The progress of the productive forces is defined by the capacity of the same quantity of direct labor (a and b) to set to work a larger mass of equipment and raw material and produce by this means a larger mass of equipment and consumer goods. Or, when λ and γ measure the progress of the productivity of labor (with λ and γ both >1):

$$1e + a\lambda h = pe$$
$$1e + b\gamma h = qc$$

Within this very general framework I established the following set of propositions:

1. A dynamic equilibrium is possible, provided only that labor-power ($a + b$) is distributed between the two departments in suitable proportions.

2. The pace of accumulation (measured by the growth in the production of equipment) conditions the level of employment (a conclusion opposite to that assumed by conventional economics).

3. Dynamic equilibrium presupposes that the consumer goods produced during one phase are purchased during

that same phase and the equipment goods produced during one phase are purchased at the beginning of the next. Since the surplus-value generated during one phase cannot be realized until the next phase, dynamic equilibrium requires centralized and correct management of credit.

4. If the entire economy is reduced to these two departments, dynamic equilibrium demands that there be an increase in wages, to be determined in a proportion that combines λ and γ.

5. If real wages do not follow their necessary progression, equilibrium is possible only if a third department, for unproductive consumption of surplus-value, develops parallel with Departments I and II.

1. AN ILLUSTRATION WITH A SIMPLE MODEL OF ACCUMULATION

The relation between the two departments of production can be expressed in terms of physical quantities:

$$\text{Department I} \quad 1e + 4h \rightarrow 3e$$
$$\text{Department II} \quad 1e + 4h \rightarrow 6c$$

Constant capital inputs are given directly in capital goods units e, direct labor inputs in hours h; outputs are given in capital goods units e for Department I and in consumption units c for Department II. In this example, it will be noted that the organic composition is the same in both Departments.

It is assumed that the product of labor is shared between the proletarian and the capitalist in identical proportions in the two Departments (identical rates of surplus-value). It is also assumed that wages constitute the sole source of demand for consumer goods c, i.e., that the purchasing power incorporated in the remuneration of labor enables the entire output of Department II to be absorbed during each successive phase described. On the other hand, the entire surplus-value is "saved," in order to finance gross investment (replacement and additions), i.e., the purchasing power incorporated in the surplus-value generated during one phase enables the installation of the capital goods necessary to maintain the dynamic equilibrium of the next phase.

As to dynamic equilibrium, we define the progress achieved between one phase and the next by the rate of increase of labor productivity (the output divided by the input of direct labor). For example, if productivity in each Department doubles between one phase and the next, the technology for Phase 2 will be given as follows:

$$\text{Department I} \quad 2e + 4h \rightarrow 6e$$
$$\text{Department II} \quad 2e + 4h \rightarrow 12c$$

The same quantity of direct labor utilizes twice the quantity of capital goods, raw materials, etc., to produce a doubled output. The physical organic compositions are doubled.

How, under these conditions, can equilibrium be maintained from one phase to the next? Let us assume that the quantity of labor available in the society ($120h$) and available stock of capital goods ($30e$) are given from the outset. Their distribution between the two Departments, the rate of surplus-value and the rate of growth (the surplus production in I over replacement needs) are simultaneously interdependent. For example, we have:

Phase 1	Capital Equipment		Necessary Labor		Surplus Labor		Output
Department 1	$20e$	+	$40h$	+	$40h$	→	$60e$
Department II	$10e$	+	$20h$	+	$20h$	→	$60c$
TOTAL	$30e$			$120h$			

Here, the output of Department I during Phase 1 is twice what is necessary to replace the capital equipment and makes it possible to obtain during Phase 2 an output which is itself doubled. We verify that the proportions 2/3–1/3 which represent the distribution of the productive forces between I and II and a surplus-value rate of 100 percent, i.e., unchanged (hence double real wages) are the conditions of dynamic equilibrium, where Phase 2 is expressed in the following way:

Phase 2	Capital Equipment		Necessary Labor		Surplus Labor		Output
Department 1	$40e$	+	$40h$	+	$40h$	→	$120e$
Department II	$20e$	+	$20h$	+	$20h$	→	$120c$
TOTAL	$60e$		$120h$				

Note that the purchasing power incorporated in the wages corresponding to 120 hours of labor (of which $60h$ is necessary labor) should make it possible to purchase $60c$ during Phase 1 and $120c$ during Phase 2, i.e., that real wages should double in the same way as labor productivity. Capital equipment output, being doubled between one phase and the next, finds an outlet in the following phase. We note that the rate of increase of available capital equipment governs the total quantity of labor used and not the reverse. This is a very important point: the accumulation of capital governs employment and not the reverse (as claimed by bourgeois economics in general and marginalism in particular). Here, by the very choice of assumptions, the volume of employment remains unchanged from one period to another. Under the assumption of an increase in the working population, for instance, a natural increase, the rate of accumulation does not make full employment possible.

This very simple model illustrates the nature of the objective relation between the value of labor-power and the development level of the productive forces in the capitalist mode of production. Nothing is gained by using a common denominator so as to be able to add up the inputs, by substituting prices for values in the computation (equalization of the profit rate which is, here in any case, equal to the rate of surplus-value, the organic compositions being the same in both Departments), or by introducing more complicated assumptions: different organic compositions and/or different increases in productivity in the two Departments.

The conditions of equilibrium, for example, can obviously be expressed in homogeneous terms. Assuming the unit price of c to be $1F$, that of e, $2F$, and the wage rate per hour $0.50F$, the surplus-value (here equal to the profit) being obtained as the difference, we have the situation shown in Phase 1. For the following phase, if the money wage rate remains the same, the prices of the products are reduced by half, productivity having doubled (see Phase 2). Note that there is no difficulty of absorption. For the absorption of consumer goods, the wages paid in each phase ($60F$) make it possible to purchase the entire output of Department II in the same phase: in the first phase, $60c$ at $1F$ per unit; in the second phase, $120c$ at $0.50F$ per unit.

Phase 1	Capital Equipment	Wages	Surplus-Value	Output
Department I	$20e \times 2 = 40F$	$80h \times 0.5 = 40F$	$40F$	$60e \times 2 = 120F$
Department II	$10e \times 2 = 20F$	$40h \times 0.5 = 20F$	$20F$	$60c \times 1 = 60F$
TOTAL	$60F$	$60F$	$60F$	$180F$

Phase 2				
Department I	$40e \times 1 = 40F$	$80h \times 0.5 = 40F$	$40F$	$120e \times 1 = 120F$
Department II	$20e \times 2 = 20F$	$40h \times 0.5 = 20F$	$20F$	$120c \times 0.5 = 60F$
TOTAL	$60F$	$60F$	$60F$	$180F$

A useful observation at this point is that the capital equipment produced during one phase does not have the same use-value as did the capital equipment used in its production. With the $20e$ installed during Phase 1, not $60e$ of the same type but $60e$ of a new type were produced. For instance, with steam engines would be produced, not more steam engines, but electric motors. Otherwise, there would be no way to understand how, with the same type of capital equipment, its efficiency would be doubled in the following phase. If the capital equipments were the same, their efficiency would be the same; that is to say, the same ratio of capital equipment to direct labor. If the same quantity of direct labor can set in motion twice the value in capital equipment in order to produce twice as much output, it means that the equipment is different, new, and more efficient.

This observation allows us to distinguish between a model of intensive expanded reproduction from an extensive model. In the latter, the same capital equipment is produced, but in increasing quantity (such extensive expanded reproduction requires for its service a proportionally increased amount of labor). In the—more interesting—intensive model considered here this is no longer necessarily the case. (A general algebraic model of expanded reproduction is formulated in the Appendix to this chapter.)

2. REALIZATION OF THE SURPLUS-PRODUCT AND THE ACTIVE FUNCTION OF CREDIT

From this general scheme of expanded reproduction I have thus deduced a first important conclusion, namely, that dynamic equilibrium requires the existence of a *credit system* that places at the capitalists' disposal the income that they will realize during the next phase. This demonstration established the status of the Marxist theory of money and gives precise content to the Marxist (anti-quantity-theory) proposition that the supply of money adjusts itself to the demand for money (to social need), by linking this social need to the conditions for accumulation. How important this proposition is remains unperceived by those theorists who do not dare to *continue* Marx's work, but prefer to confine themselves to *expounding* it. Moreover, this precise integration of credit into the theory of accumulation is the *only* answer to the "market question" raised by Rosa Luxemburg.[1]

3. GIVEN THE HYPOTHESIS OF UNCHANGING REAL WAGES, IS ACCUMULATION POSSIBLE?

What happens with the equations of expanded-reproduction when real wages do not increase at the same rate as productivity; for example, when the real wage per hour remains unchanged? There are only two sets of mathematical solutions to the problem: an absurd one corresponding to Tugan-Baranovsky's "round-about" approach, and a realistic one, introducing the consumption of the surplus-value.

Joining in the debates concerning markets and the trade cycle as early as the beginning of the twentieth century, Tugan-Baranovsky considered a succession of phases in dynamic equilibrium is spite of stagnation in real hourly wages in *The Industrial Crises in England*, published in Germany in 1901. The additional equipment produced in the course of each phase, and in increasing quantity as a result of increased productivity, is allocated to Department I in the following phase in order to produce other equipment, capital, and so on indefinitely, while Department II only expands insofar as the use of the additional equipment requires a quantitative increase in labor, since the hourly wage rate remains unchanged. In the next example, where productivity doubles from one phase to the next in each of the two Departments, we have:

Phase 2	Capital Equipment	Necessary Labor	Surplus-Labor		Output
Department I	50e	100h	(25h, 75h)	→	150e
Department II	10e	20h	(5h, 15h)	→	60c
TOTAL	60e	120h	(30h, 90h)		

Phase 3					
Department I	137.5e	137.5h	(17.5h, 120h)	→	412.5e
Department II	12.5e	12.5h	(1.5h, 11h)	→	75.0c
TOTAL	150.0e	150.0h	(19.0h, 131h)		

The utilization of 60e produced in the course of Phase 1 requires 120h of direct labor during Phase 2. The labor, with its real wage unchanged, is able to purchase 60c, which require only 10e and 20h of direct labor. The remaining equipment (50e) will enable 150e to be produced. This equipment will require in Phase 3 an extra labor of 150h, which combine to produce an output in Department II of 75c (which only requires 12.5e and 12.5h). Equilibrium is achieved from one phase to the next in spite of the stagnation in the real hourly wage combined with the growth in productivity (with a doubling in each department from one phase to the next—both in labor productivity and in the physical organic composition). Equilibrium is obtained through a distortion in the distribution of the productive forces in favor of Department I and the increase in the rate of surplus-value, as follows:

	Phase 1	Phase 2	Phase 3
Organic Composition (Index)	$30e/120h$	$60e/120h$	$150e/150h$
	100	200	400
Productivity in Department I (Index)	$60e/80h$	$150e/100h$	$412.5e/137.5h$
	100	200	400
Productivity in Department II (Index)	$60c/40h$	$60c/20h$	$75c/12.5h$
	100	200	400
Distribution I/(I+II)	2/3	5/6	0.91
Rate of Surplus-value (percent)	100	300	690

This "roundabout" solution is absurd since the balance
between consumption and capital equipment must be obtained
from one phase to the next and cannot be indefinitely postponed.
If each phase corresponds to the life of the capital equipment, this
period coincides exactly with the "planning" period for investment decisions. Capital goods will be produced in the course of
one phase only if in the following phase the output of consumer
goods which they bring about finds an outlet. Thus, in fact, if
hourly wages are stagnant, there will be an overproduction crisis
as from Phase 2, with the equipment produced in Phase 1 remaining unused, while that proportion of it that does get used will only
give rise to a reduced demand for labor. This is the Keynesian
problem and the source of the Great Depression: the system has
broken down (available equipment and unemployment) and can
only be started up again by a rise in wages.

Oddly, the Tugan-Baranovsky solution, absurd in a real capitalism, can be envisaged in the hypothetical case of a planned sta-
tism, which would have the means to allow itself to push ever outward the consumption horizon that, under capitalism, governs
profitability and investment decisions. Indeed, that was the case
in the Soviet system during the Stalinist epoch.

The absurd part of it can be avoided if the surplus-value is consumed. In our very simple scheme, the entire surplus-value is

"saved"; but if we assume that a constant proportion of it is consumed, there will be no change in the nature of the equilibria. Hence, if real hourly wages remain stagnant or increase at a lower rate than productivity, an increasing proportion of the surplus-value must be consumed in order to maintain a dynamic equilibrium. For there are no "insurmountable" contradictions—the thesis of catastrophic collapse, of a "general crisis," etc.—but only different alternative ways of overcoming them: capitalist alternatives that preserve the essential features of the system and socialist alternatives that go beyond them.

Under capitalism the question is to be answered through one of the three following solutions:

1. The first "solution"—the individual consumption of an increasing proportion of the surplus-value by the capitalist—is not "normal" since competition among capitalists requires "savings" and the ideology of the system, which reflects the features of the capitalist mode, is opposed to it.

2. The second "solution" is one discovered by the central system itself in order to overcome its contradictions. We have already noted that there are no "insurmountable" contradictions—the theory of catastrophic collapse, of "general crisis," etc.—but only different alternatives to overcome them: those of capitalism that maintain the essential features of the system and those of socialism, which supersede them right from the start. Monopolistic competition, the inclusion of "selling costs" in the price of the product, and the subsequent development of tertiary parasitism, which were well described long ago by Chamberlin and Joan Robinson, constitute, as Baran and Sweezy have said, the "spontaneous" solution of the system.[2]

3. The third "solution" involves direct intervention by the state in the absorption: public, civil, and military expenditure. Paul Baran's great intuition was to understand that henceforth the analysis of dynamic equilibrium could not be made within the framework of the "pure" two-sector model but within a new framework—with three sectors (the third sector in fact being the state, consumer of an increasing proportion of the surplus). This analysis, which corresponds to reality, required the introduction of a concept wider than that of surplus-value and directly linked with the productivity of productive labor. The concept is that of surplus.

Does the introduction of these "solutions," the third in particular, remove the objective status of labor-power? The answer is yes, for those who regard this status from an economistic point of view. But in actual fact, these "solutions" remind us only of the existence of a dialectic between subjective and objective forces; for state intervention must be placed within the context of the class struggle that gives it its meaning.

Dialectic does not mean juxtaposition of autonomous elements. Class struggle, in all its varied manifestations outlined here, does not "reveal" the objective necessities of equilibrium by a lucky chance. Class struggle modifies the objective conditions. The model is necessarily unilateral, but reality is not. The results of class struggle alter the conditions of the "model": they act upon the allocation of resources, the rates of growth of productivity, etc. Objective conditions and subjective forces act and react upon each other.

A final remark: the preceding analysis of dynamic equilibrium did not contain assumptions regarding the trend of the profit rate. We will return to this question later, in relation to the stages of the evolution of the capitalist system and the related question of the falling rate of profit. I will not here enter into the discussions about the "law of the falling tendency of the rate of profit." Following Paul Sweezy, I have in my turn dared to offer several reflections going beyond what Marx wrote on the question. Thus I entered the discussion to suggest that the facts that can be acknowledged concerning changes in the profit rate be placed in the context of a concrete historical framework defining successive phases characterized by particular combinations of the indicators (*lambda*, λ, and *gamma*, γ) of the growth of productivity in each of the two sections modeled in Marx's line of argument.

4. FROM PRICES OF PRODUCTION
TO MARKET PRICES

As the competition among segments of capital is enough to account for the transformation of values into prices of production, we have now to consider a third family of operative realities, which in their turn transform prices of production into market prices. The first element to be considered here is the existence of oligopolies, which wipe out the liberal hypothesis of "competition." These oligopolies, which have defined contemporary capitalism since the end of the nineteenth century, are positioned to bleed off monopoly rents from the overall mass of surplus-value, guaranteeing them rates of profit higher than those obtained by the segments of capital subordinate to them. The contributions of Baran, Sweezy, and Magdoff have brought about a qualitative advance in this domain. They alone allow an understanding of the nature of capitalism in our time, both its tendency to stagnate and the ways in which it tries to overcome that tendency (especially financialization).

Extending that analysis, I have put forward the thesis that the advanced degree of centralization of capital, henceforward characteristic of contemporary capitalism, made it worthwhile to speak, for the first time, of a system of generalized, global-

THE FUNDAMENTAL STATUS OF THE LAW OF VALUE

ized, and financialized oligopolies—the basis for the crystallization of a collective imperialism of the triad of the United States, Europe, and Japan.[3]

The second intervening element in the determination of market prices calls for a theoretical analysis of the functions of the monetary standard. Marx here puts forward an expanded view of great interest concerning the interlinking of the "standard commodity" (gold) and the role of credit in creating and destroying money. I likewise have put forward several theses about this subject under the new conditions in which the metallic standard has been generally abandoned.[4] The fact remains that human societies—on account of their alienation (in this instance, the market alienation proper to capitalism) always need a "fetish." Gold, in the last analysis, remains that of our "modern" world, as is seen at moments of accumulation crisis—our present moment, for example.

A third family of disparate elements, whether they define a general conjuncture (times of easy growth and times of sharpening competition among capitals) or special conjunctions ("new" products versus products whose growth potential is becoming exhausted), enters into the determination of observed market prices.

The absolute empiricism that is the standpoint of vulgar economics, dominant in Anglo-Saxon cultures even more than elsewhere, claims to draw "laws" allowing the understanding of economic life directly from the observation of immediate realities (prices such as they are). Its failure—as our subsequent consideration of Sraffa's model will show—simply reveals the ideological nature of vulgar economics, reduced to chatter designed to legitimize the activities of capital.

5. THE UNAVOIDABLE DETOUR
BY WAY OF VALUE

What does the law of value state? That products, when they are commodities, possess value; that this value is measurable; that the yardstick for measuring it is the quantity of abstract labor socially necessary to produce them; and, finally, that this quantity is the sum of the quantities of labor, direct and indirect (transferred), that are used in the process of production. The concept of the commodity and the existence of the law of value, formulated in this way, are inseparably interconnected.

What does the law of value *not* state? That commodities are exchanged in proportion to their values; and that direct labor is present labor, whereas indirect labor is past labor crystallized in the means of production. (Volume II of *Capital* is based on the fact that the production of the means of production and the production of consumer goods are not successive in time, but simultaneous, this simultaneity defining the social division of labor in its most fundamental aspect.)

Possessing a certain value and being exchanged at that rate are two different notions. Marx says that, in the capitalist mode, commodities are exchanged in accordance with relations defined by their prices of production. Is this a contradiction? Does it mean that making a detour by way of value is pointless? My view is that neither is so.

Prices of production result from a synthesis of the law of value, on the one hand, and the law of competition among capitals, on the other. The first-mentioned factor, the more fundamental of the two, would cause exchange to take place in accordance with value in a mode of production reduced to the sole reality of domination by the commodity, that is, simple commodity production. This mode does not exist in history. The capitalist mode, which cannot be reduced to this, is characterized by the presence, alongside domination by the commodity, of the fragmentation of capital and competition among capitals (and capitalists). Visible reality, in the form of prices of production, results from the combining of these two laws, which are situated on different levels.

We say that prices of production result from the combined action of the two laws. Can this combination be expressed in a quantified transformation formula? In Volume III of *Capital* Marx does this, in his usual way, by giving numerical examples of various possible cases. He does not put forward successive approximations, but confines himself to a first approximation: constant capital stays measured in value, not in price. One can, without difficulty, solve the problem of transformation in an elegant way, without successive approximations, by means of a system of simultaneous equations. Is this operation legitimate? Certainly it is.

It cannot be said that value is a category of the process of production whereas price belongs to the process of circulation. Value and price are both categories of the process as a whole. Actually, value is realized, and consequently exists, only through exchange. It is in this overall process that concrete labor is transformed into abstract labor, and complex (compound) labor into simple labor.

The only condition for transformation is that it should be possible to reduce concrete wage-labor to a quantity of abstract labor. In fact the actual tendency of capitalism is indeed—by subjecting labor to the machine and downgrading labor skill on a mass scale—to reduce concrete forms of labor to abstract labor.

The question of transformation has been obscured by the fact that the writers who first tried to carry through the operation begun in Volume III of *Capital* also wanted to solve a problem that was easily shown to be insoluble: transforming values into prices while retaining equality between the rates of profit resulting from the equations establishing the production prices and that rate of profit expressed in value and derived directly from the rate of surplus-value.

If we abandon this requirement, we find no difficulty in transforming values into prices. Is the fact that the rate of profit necessarily differs from the rate of surplus-value an embarrassing fact? On the contrary, it is normal for these two rates to differ: indeed, this result of transformation is one of the essential discoveries of Marxism.

In the "transparent" modes of exploitation, the rate of exploitation is immediately obvious: the serf works for three days on his or her own land and for three days on the master's. Neither the serf nor the lord is blind to this fact. But the capitalist mode of exploitation is opaque. On the one hand, the proletarian sells his labor-power, but seems to be selling labor, and is paid for the eight hours of work put in, not just for the four that would be necessary for maintenance; on the other hand the bourgeois realizes a profit that is calculated in relation to the capital owned, not to the labor exploited, so that this capital seems to the capitalist to be productive.

I have ascribed fundamental importance to this difference between the transparency of precapitalist exploitation and the opacity of the extortion of surplus-value under capitalism, and have based upon this distinction a series of propositions dealing respectively with (a) the different contents of precapitalist ideology (alienation in nature) and capitalist ideology (market alienation), and (b) the different relations between base and superstructure, with dominance by the ideological instance in all the precapitalist modes and, contrariwise, direct domination by the economic base in capitalist mode. Thereby I have related the appearance of "economic laws," and so of "economic science," to the capitalist mode.

Bourgeois economic science (neoclassical, i.e., vulgar, economics) tries to grasp these laws directly, on the basis of what is immediately obvious. It therefore takes capital for what it seems to the capitalist to be, that is, a factor of production, productive in itself, with labor as another factor of production.

6. Is an Empiricist Approach
to Accumulation Possible?

The strictly empiricist philosophical mind-set of the Anglo-Saxon world, transmitted to all contemporary vulgar economics, means that only observable facts ("prices," such as they are) count toward the direct deduction of "laws" allowing one to understand the mechanisms of the reproduction of the system and of its expansion. For the "professional" economist, an empiricist and nothing but an empiricist, a detour by way of value is burdensome and useless.

One might confine oneself to replying that to understand capitalism means not only to understand its economic laws but also to understand the link between these laws and the general conditions of social reproduction, that is, the way its ideological instance functions in relation to its base. The concept of value is a key concept, enabling one to grasp this reality in its full richness. Those who carry out the reduction, which I here condemn, always end up by conceiving socialism as nothing but "capitalism without capitalists."

However, this argument, though sound, is not the only one available. We will, in fact, see that the empiricist treatment of the question, which "economizes" that "burdensome and useless detour" (for it) by directly apprehending reality as expressed in "market prices," loses itself in a blind alley.

7. Sraffa's Schema

In Sraffa's model the productive system is given (the quantities of each commodity, $1, 2, \ldots i, \ldots n$, and the techniques used to produce them, including the inputs of direct labor), as is the real wage (the quantity of various goods that the hourly wage enables the wage earner to buy). Consequently, the relative prices and the rate of profit are determined in static equilibrium. The difference between the two methods is situated on two planes, which must be carefully distinguished: (a) the substitution of prices for values; and (b) the adoption of a system of production with n branches instead of the two departments specializing in the production, respectively, of equipment goods and of consumer goods.

Let us assume that there are two lines of production, (1) and (2), each of which produces both producer goods and consumer goods, and that a_{ij} = the coefficients of inputs necessary for the production of these goods, p_1 and p_2 = their unit prices; w = the wage rate (the quantities of labor being assigned by the coefficients a_{01} and a_{02}); and r = the rate of profit. We then have:

$$(a_{11}p_1 + a_{12}p_2 + a_{01}w)\,(1 + r) = p_1$$

$$(a_{21}p_1 + a_{22}p_2 + a_{02}w)\,(1 + r) = p_2$$

To this system corresponds the following system of values:

$$a_{11}v_1 + a_{12}v_2 + a_{01} = v_1$$

$$a_{21}v_1 + a_{22}v_2 + a_{02} = v_2$$

Let it be remembered that since the two products (1) and (2) are not destined by nature, one for use as equipment and the other for consumption, this system does not describe an equilibrium of supply and demand for each department. The conditions for *that* equilibrium, which are assumed to be achieved, are external to the model.

We define two parameters of improvement in productivity, π_1 and π_2, specific to each of the branches (1) and (2). Let us assume, for simplicity, that it is the same, π, in both cases. Let us go on to assume that the system of values for Phase 1 is as follows:

$$0.2v_1 + 0.4v_2 + 0.4 = v_1$$

$$0.5v_1 + 0.1v_2 + 0.6 = v_2$$

from which we get:

$$v_1 = 1.15, \text{ and } v_2 = 1.30$$

Assuming that the same quantity of direct labor becomes capable of setting to work twice as much equipment and raw material and, for simplicity, in the same proportions a_{ij} so as to provide twice the quantity of end products (that is, if $\pi = 0.5$), we have for Phase 2:

$$0.4v'_1 + 0.8v'_2 + 0.4 = 2v'_1$$

$$1.0v'_1 + 0.2v'_2 + 0.6 = 2v'_2$$

from which we get:

$$v'_1 = 0.58 \text{ and } v'_2 = 0.65$$

The table below will then show the evolution of the system of values obtained with the same global quantity of labor, left unchanged.

The results, meaning the increase in the net product (from 1.00 to 2.00) are independent of distribution (no assumptions having been made regarding wages or the rate of profit).

	Phase 1	Phase 2
Production	$1.0v_1 + 1.0v_2 = 2.45$	$2.0v'_1 + 2.0v'_2 = 4.92$
– Productive consumption	$0.7v_1 + 0.5v_2 = 1.45$	$1.4v'_1 + 1.0v'_2 = 2.92$
= Net Product	$0.3v_1 + 0.5v_2 = 1.00$	$0.6v'_1 + 1.0v'_2 = 2.00$

Rising productivity can be expressed by falling prices while nominal incomes remain unchanged or by nominal incomes' increases with unchanged unit prices. Here prices are doubled:

$$v'_1 = 1.15 \qquad v'_2 = 1.30$$

If, however, we examine the evolution of a system expressed in prices, we have to introduce an assumption regarding *the way income is distributed.*

The previous system, expressed in price terms, namely:

$$(0.2p_1 + 0.4p_2 + 0.4w)(1 + r) = p_1$$
$$(0.5p_1 + 0.1p_2 + 0.6w)(1 + r) = p_2$$

completed by an assumption regarding wages, e.g., that:

$$w = 0.2p_1 + 0.2p_2$$

can be reduced to a system of "production of commodities by means of commodities only" which here is as follows:

$$(0.28p_1 + 0.48p_2)(1 + r) = p_1$$
$$(0.62p_1 + 0.22p_2)(1 + r) = p_2$$

the solutions of which are:
$$p_1/p_2 = 0.93$$

For the next phase the system becomes:

$$(0.4p'_1 + 0.8p'_2 + 0.4w')(1 + r') = 2p'_1$$
$$(1.0p_1 + 0.2p'_2 + 0.6w')(1 + r') = 2p'_2$$

The results (relative prices and rate of profit) will depend on the way that wages evolve. If we assume an unchanged real wage, that is, if

$$w' = w = 0.2p'_1 + 0.2p'_2$$

the reduced system becomes:

$$(0.24p'_1 + 0.44p'_2)(1 + r') = p'_1$$

$$(0.56p'_1 + 0.16p'_2)(1 + r') = p'_2$$

the solutions of which are $p'_1/p'_2 = 0.98$, from which we get the comparative table, established in price terms, given below:

	Phase 1	Phase 2
Production	$1.0p_1 + 1.0p_2 = 2.08$	$2.0p'_1 + 2.0p'_2 = 4.04$
– Productive consumption	$0.7p_1 + 0.5p_2 = 1.24$	$1.4p'_1 + 1.0p'_2 = 2.42$
= Net Product	$0.3p_1 + 0.5p_2 = 0.84$	$0.6p'_1 + 1.0p'_2 = 1.62$
of which, wages	$0.2p_1 + 0.2p_2 = 0.42$	$0.2p'_1 + 0.2p'_2 = 0.40$
and profits	$0.1p_1 + 0.3p_2 = 0.42$	$0.4p'_1 + .8p'_2 = 1.22$

It will be noted that comparison between the two phases is obscured by the fact that the solution of the system gives relative prices, p_1/p_2 and p'_1/p'_2, which differ according to the evolution of wages. We do know, from our assumption, that the system of Phase 2 will enable us to obtain, with the same total quantity of labor, twice as much physical product (use-values) from (1) and (2). But if we assume $p_1 = p'_1 = 1$, we have p_2 unequal to p'_2, since p_1/p_2 and p'_1/p'_2 both depend on the way distribution takes place. Here $p_2 = 1.08$ and $p'_2 = 1.02$.

The net product, which is the measurement of the growth in value that is independent of distribution (in my model, this net product increases in value terms from 1.00 to 2.00), here increases from 0.84 to 1.62 (a growth rate of 93 percent) when we analyze the evolution of the system in price terms, with the given assumption regarding wages.

It is because of these uncertainties in measurement of the development of the productive forces in price terms that we should prefer models constructed in terms of value, the only certain standard.

The major defect of analysis in price terms compared with analysis in terms of value is not due to the "open" character of Sraffa's model (meaning that the dynamic equilibrium of supply and demand for each product—equipment goods and consumer goods—is not formulated as an internal condition of the model but simply assumed to be related externally), in contrast to the "closed" (full circle) character of Marx's model (in which the equilibrium in question is formalized in the model itself). This defect is due to the substitution of prices, which depend on distribution, for values, which do not so depend. This means that the concept of improvement in the productivity of labor (as the measure of the development of the productive forces), which is perfectly objective in Marx's practice (it does not depend on the rate of surplus-value), is no longer objective in Sraffa's model or in any other model constructed in price terms.

Furthermore, the Sraffian framework does not lend itself to analysis of the conditions for dynamic equilibrium, since, unlike Marx's framework, it is not concerned with the equilibrium of supply and demand for each type of product. It is therefore impossible to deduce from it the propositions set out above concerning expanded reproduction. What it offers is a meager empirical model, which serves at best to describe an evolution that has been observed, but not to infer from this any laws of evolution.

A system defined directly in price terms is also perfectly determined—in the sense that relative prices and the rate of profit are determined—once the rate of real wages is given.

But then there arises the question of a standard, which Sraffa, in the Ricardian tradition, defines like this: is there a standard that would leave the net product unchanged while distribution (w or r) changed independently? The answer to this question is no. Let us see why this is so.

Sraffa does not analyze the system as Marx does. He excludes labor-power from the productive process, in order to consider wages not as the value of labor-power but as a distribution category. This is why he describes the system in the following form:

$$(0.2p_1 + 0.4p_2)(1 + r) + 0.4w = p_1$$

$$(0.5p_1 + 0.1p_2)(1 + r) + 0.6w = p_2$$

He further proposes, as we know, that we select as our standard the price of the net product:

$$0.3p_1 + 0.5p_2 = 1$$

With this standard, r and w are in a linear relationship that is independent of p_1 and p_2:

$$r = R(1 - w)$$

With this standard, r and w are in a linear relationship, whereas any arbitrarily chosen standard gives a relationship between r and w that is neither linear nor monotonic, and is described by a curve (see graph on opposite page).

But is this standard any better than others? Not so at all: (a) because this standard presupposes Sraffa's treatment of wages: if the wage is integrated in the productive process as variable capital, the standard varies when w varies: it is no longer independent of prices; (b) because, even in Sraffa's formulation, since the net product changes with the passage of time (the result of growth), the standard is not independent of prices but is elastic.

If then we reintegrate w in the productive process, as we should, whatever the standard being used, we get three equations and four unknowns (p_1, p_2, r, and w). It is still possible to express r as a function of w, but the relation is no longer linear, nor even of necessity a monotonic decreasing one.

The fundamental question underlying the dispute over whether to choose value as the standard, or something else, is that of how to measure, precisely and objectively, the progress of the productive forces.

The value standard, on the other hand, enables us to measure the progress of the productive forces from one phase to another; that was why Marx chose it.

It is not fair to Marx to reduce his proposition that value should be chosen as the standard of prices to the argument that this standard "works"—that is, that with it transformation is possible. The debate on transformation remains secondary, and however much ink it has caused to flow, it is in no sense primordial.

Marx was actually seeking an instrument by which the development of the productive forces could be measured. This instrument is value. In fact, the quantity of socially necessary labor is, in the last analysis, society's only "wealth"—and value is independent of distribution.

This value standard means comparing the progress from one system (0) to another—(1), (2), etc.—along the Y-axis w. Along this axis $r = 0$, and wages w absorb the entire net product. The system that maximizes w for $r = 0$ maximizes income, or else minimizes the socially necessary labor time needed to produce a given amount of use-values. It corresponds, therefore, to more efficient, more highly developed productive forces.

Sraffa's standard, on the other hand, means comparing the systems along the X-axis r. For $w = 0$, $r = R$, and profit absorbs the entire product. Assuming w different from zero does not affect the conclusion since Sraffa cancels the wage by replacing it with the goods consumed by the wage earner. Sraffa therefore compares

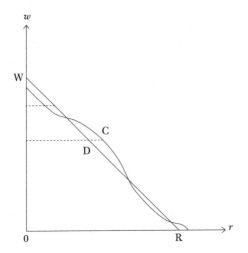

systems along a horizontal line parallel to the z axis, starting somewhere on the vertical w axis. The system that maximizes the rate of profit R will be considered the best. Isn't that the same thing? Not necessarily. The result of the two methods of comparison would be the same only if the two curves (0) and (1) did not intersect. If they do intersect, then it is possible that the system that maximizes w does not maximize r.

Why is this? Because, along the Y-axis $(r = 0)$ comparison between the systems takes into consideration simultaneously (for a system with two products) the four coefficients a_{11}, a_{12}, a_{21}, and a_{22}, corresponding to the commodity inputs, and the two coefficients a_{01} and a_{02}, defining the inputs of direct labor. The productive systems become (for $r = 0$):

$$a_{11}p_1 + a_{12}p_2 + wa_{01} = p_1$$

$$a_{21}p_1 + a_{22}p_2 + wa_{02} = p_2$$

and the prices p are then similar to the values.

If, however, we compare the productive systems along the X-axis for which $w = 0$, this means taking into consideration only the first four coefficients (production of commodities by means of commodities, and not by means of commodities plus direct labor) and leaving out the two coefficients of input of direct labor. The systems then become (for $w = 0$):

$$(a_{11}p_1 + a_{12}p_2)(1 + r) = p_1$$

$$(a_{21}p_1 + a_{22}p_2)(1 + r) = p_2$$

The value standard is superior because this standard alone considers production as the resultant of *all* the technical coefficients that describe it.

The conclusion of this analysis is fundamental: that social system that maximizes the rate of profit (for a given level of wages) does not necessarily maximize the development of the productive forces (the reduction of social labor time).

There is no way of doing without the theory of value. This theory alone enables us to link all the economic magnitudes (prices and incomes) to a common denominator—value, that is, the quantity of socially necessary labor, which is independent of the rules of distribution (exploitation, competition, and so on), and to do this both for characterizing a given phase (static synchronic analysis) and for measuring change from one phase to another (dynamic diachronic analysis) of the progress of the productive forces.

If a single standard is chosen to describe two systems, successive or simultaneous, there is a relation between w and r that is illustrated (see page 41) either by two curves of type C or by one curve C plus one straight line D.

In the system of Sraffa there can exist no common standard for two systems. In that system, wages being replaced by their equivalent (the consumption goods destined for workers), labor disappears from the production equations: commodities are then only produced by means of commodities without intervening labor (which remains underlying); the surplus being entirely attributable to capital, which becomes the only factor of production! We have here reached the highest stage of alienation: commodities (including subsistence goods for workers) have children (a larger quantity of commodities) without the intervention of labor as such. This supreme alienation is comparable to that of the financier who, making money by means of money, regards money as in itself productive (see chapter two). Or, even further, material inputs are made to disappear, replaced by their equivalent in past labor. Then in the system will appear only one factor, dated labor falling back on the factor "productive time" à la Böhm-Bawerk.

All post-Marxian economics has tried—in order to get rid of Marx—to put the origin of "progress" somewhere other than in social labor. To that end, it has invented specific productivities of "the factors of production," or reduced these to that of the "commodity" (Sraffa: "commodities produced by means of commodities"), or to that of money (money produces money), or to that of time ("time is money," Böhm-Bawerk's discounting of the future), or—today—that of "science" ("cognitive capitalism," descended from the marginal efficiency of capital as it was understood by Keynes). All these are nothing but forms of the basic alienation proper to conventional bourgeois social thought.

Marx had filled out his critique of capitalist reality with a critique of the writings that aimed to legitimize capitalist practice, whether those produced by the great classics, who founded modern thought in the domain of the new political economy (Smith, Ricardo), or of those from the vulgar economics already present in his day (Bastiat and others). Critique of the post-Marxian economists is no less necessary. It has been carried out by several good Marxists who have thrown off the yoke of exegesis. In this regard, the contributions of Baran, Sweezy, and Magdoff have been crucial. Let me point here to my own contribution to critique of the best attempts of conventional economics to extend the classics (Keynes, Sraffa) and also my critique of the new forms of vulgar economics (which I called "the witchcraft of modern times").[5]

8. ECONOMIC LAWS AND THE CLASS STRUGGLE

The schema of expanded reproduction thus seems to reveal that precise economic laws do exist, which, like any other laws, have an objective existence, that is, impose themselves willy-nilly on everyone.

To conclude, the importance of Volume II of *Capital, as it stands*, is essential: it shows that, in the capitalist mode, social reproduction appears first and foremost as *economic* reproduction. Whereas in the precapitalist modes, in which exploitation was transparent, reproduction implied direct intervention from the level of the superstructure, that is not so here. This qualitative difference needs to be emphasized.

There has been no question, so far, of the class struggle. This is, indeed, absent from the direct discourse of Volume II of *Capital*.

"Economic determinism" was foreign to Marx, but not so to historical Marxism. A linear economic determinism, linked to a scientistic philosophical vision of "progress," was predominant in the Second International and became even more dominant when social democracy, after the Second World War, abandoned its claim to derivation from Marx.

One attitude that can be taken in this connection is that the class struggle setting bourgeoisie and proletariat against each other over the division of the product (the rate of surplus-value) is subordinate to economic laws. The class struggle can, at most, only reveal the equilibrium rate that is objectively necessary. It occupies, in this context, a position comparable to that of the "invisible hand" of bourgeois economics. The language of the "universal harmony" of social interests is replaced by that of the "objective necessities of progress."

What we have here is a reduction of Marxism to the so-called Marxist (or, rather, Marxian) political economy that is fashionable in the English-speaking world under the name of "Marxian economics." According to this view, there are economic laws, which constitute objective necessities, irrespective of the class struggle.

On such a basis, however, it is no longer possible to conceive of a classless society in the true sense, since it appears as a society identical with class society. The progress of the productive forces continues to dominate it, just as this progress has been dominant throughout history. This progress has its own laws: an ever more intensified division of labor, in the form we know well. Capitalism is seen as guilty only of not being able to carry forward the march of progress effectively enough. As for those writings of Marx in which he criticizes sharply the shortsightedness of the philistine who cannot imagine a future in which no one is exclusively an artist or a lathe-operator, they are so much utopian daydreaming. Capitalism is seen as, basically, a model for eternity, blameworthy only for the social "wastage" constituted by the capitalists' consumption, and for the anarchy caused by competition among capitals. Socialism will put an end to these two abuses by organizing, on the basis of state-centralized ownership of the means of production, a system of "rational planning."

How are we to arrive at this statist mode of production—the highest stage of evolution, a wise submission to "objective laws" for the greater good of society as a whole? By the road of reformism: trade unions, by imposing a "social contract" governing the distribution of the gains of productivity, prepare the way for the formal expropriation of the unnecessary capitalists, after having first served as a school of management for the cadres and elites who represent the proletariat and whose task it is to organize and command.

There is a second possible attitude. Reacting against this type of analysis, one proclaims the supremacy of the class struggle. Wage levels, it is held, result not from the objective laws of expanded reproduction, but directly from the conflict between classes. Accumulation adjusts itself, if it can, to the outcome of this struggle—and, if it can't, the system suffers crisis, that's all.

I here put forward four theses concerning the linkage among the (economic) "laws" of capitalistic accumulation, on one side, and the social struggles, in the broadest sense, on the other. By that, I mean the totality of social and political struggles and conflicts, national and international.

THESIS 1: These struggles and conflicts, in all their complexity, produce "national" systems and a global system, which go from disequilibrium to disequilibrium without ever tending toward the ideal equilibrium formulated by conventional or Marxian (but, in my opinion, scarcely Marxist) economists.

THESIS 2: The inner logic of capitalism—maximization of the rate of profit and of the mass of surplus-value—gives rise to a tendency toward a disequilibrium favoring the possessing classes (the bourgeoisie in the widest sense) at the expense of labor incomes (of all diverse forms). Capitalist reproduction, by virtue of this fact, ought to become "impossible." And in fact, the history of capitalism is not one of "continuous growth," of a "long tranquil river" assuring continuous growth of production and consumption, flowing over accidental obstructions that are called "crises." Like Paul Sweezy, I view this history, contrariwise, as being one of long crises (1873–1945; 1971 to today and, no doubt, stretching far beyond 2010), reducing the short periods of rapid (and problem-free) growth to historical exceptions (like the "thirty great years" between 1945 and 1975).[6]

THESIS 3: Despite this permanent malaise, capitalism has managed so far to get out of its blind alleys and to invent effective ways for adapting to the demands posed by changes in the balance of social and international forces. This reminds us that the progress of the productive forces (its pace and the directions it takes) is not some independent exogenous factor, but one that results from class struggle and is embodied in production relations—that it is modulated by the ruling classes. This thesis reminds us that the Taylorism of yesterday and the automation and "technological revolution" of today are responses to working class struggle, as are also the centralization of capital, imperialism, the relocation of industries, and so on.

So long as capitalism has not been overthrown, the bourgeoisie has the last word in class struggles. This must never be forgotten. It means that unless crises lead to the overthrow of capitalism—which is always a *political* act—they must always be solved in the bourgeoisie's favor. Wages that are "too high" are eroded by inflation, until the working-class, exhausted, gives in. Or else "national unity" makes it possible to shift the burden of the crisis onto others' backs.

For a view of the matter that is not one-sided we need to appreciate that the class struggle proceeds, in the first place, from a given economic situation, reflecting the reality of a particular economic basis, but that, as long as the capitalist system still exists, this modification necessarily remains confined by the laws of economic reproduction of the system. An alteration in wages affects the rate of profit, dictates a type of reaction of the bourgeoisie that is expressed in given rates of "progress" in given directions, changes the social division of labor between the two departments, and so on. But as long as we remain within the setting of capitalism, all these modifications respect the general conditions for capitalist reproduction. In short, *the class struggle operates on an economic base and shapes the way this base is transformed within the framework of the immanent laws of the capitalist mode.*

The schemata of expanded reproduction illustrate this fundamental law that the value of labor-power is not independent of the level of development of the productive forces. The value of labor-power must rise as the productive forces develop. This is how I understand the "historical element" to which Marx refers when writing of how this value is determined. The only other logical answer to that question is the rigid determination of the value of labor-power by "subsistence" (as in Ricardo, Malthus, and Lassalle).

But this objective necessity does not result spontaneously from the functioning of capitalism. On the contrary, it constantly comes up against the real tendency inherent in capitalism, which runs counter to it. The capitalists are always trying to increase the rate of surplus-value, and this contradictory tendency is what triumphs in the end. This is how I understand what is meant by the "law of accumulation" and the "relative and absolute pauperization" by which it is manifested. Facts show the reality of this law—but on the scale of the world capitalist system, not on that of the imperialist centers considered in isolation; for whereas, at the center, real wages have risen gradually for the past century, parallel with the development of the productive forces, in the periphery the absolute pauperization of the producers exploited by capital has revealed itself in all its brutal reality. But it is there, precisely, that the pro-imperialist tendency among Marxists pulls up short. For it is from that point onward that Marxism becomes subversive. (This problem of the class struggle in relation to accumulation on the world scale will arise again in chapter four.)

Capital overcomes this contradiction by developing a "third department," the function of which is to take in hand the excess surplus-value, which cannot be absorbed in Departments I and II, owing to the inadequate increase in the real wages of the productive workers. This decisive contribution by Baran and Sweezy has never been and can never be understood by any of those who decline to analyze the immanent contradiction of capitalism in dialectical terms.

Starting in the 1930s, but above all since 1945, capitalism has recorded a gigantic transformation that has borne the share of those activities called "tertiary" to heights previously unknown. The reading of this transformation by conventional economists, including Fourastié who was the first to offer an analysis of it, is uncritical—in fact, apologetic. Ours is not.

Undoubtedly the "tertiary" has always existed, if only because no capitalist society is thinkable without a state, whose monarchical functions have a social cost, covered—outside the market— by taxes. Likewise, indubitably, the expansion of "selling costs" associated with the monopolistic competition referred to previously, along with the relative autonomization of commercial and financial activities, are those things at the origin of the accelerated growth of the "tertiary." No less important, however, is the expansion of public services (education, health, and social security) produced by successes of the people's struggles.

So without here going into the labyrinth of the activities called "tertiary"—activities of fundamentally diverse natures—I will here call attention only to the theses that I have put forward concerning the linkage between the puffing up of this "Sector III" of surplus-value absorption and the imperialist fact: the concentration of control operations over the world system by the powers making up the imperialist triad (United States, Europe, and Japan) through what I have termed "five monopolies of the triad's collective imperialism".[7]

Opposed to the strategies of capital, which endeavor to capture control over this swelling of "tertiary" activities through privatization of their management in order to open new fields into which to expand—rather by expropriation than by any new creation—are possible people's strategies of democratic control of the activities in question.

The dizzying expansion of "Department III" (complementing the Departments I and II of the analysis of accumulation put forth in *Das Kapital*), which has become *de facto* "dominant" in the sense that it comprises two-thirds or more of what conventional economics terms GDP (Gross Domestic Product), certainly calls into question the formulations of the law of value that Marx offers us. It is even here that are placed the main arguments in favor of claims that "the law of value is outdated."

THESIS 4: Capitalism only adapts to the exigencies of the unfolding of struggles and conflicts that form its history at the price of accentuating its character as destroyer of the bases of its wealth— human beings (reduced to the status of labor force/commodity) and nature (reduced in the same way to commodity status). Its first long crisis (begun in 1873) paid off with thirty years of wars and revolutions (1914–1945). Its second (begun in 1971) entered the second, necessarily chaotic, stage of its unfolding with the financial collapse of 2008, bringer of horrors and destructions that henceforth are a menace to the whole human race. Capitalism has become an obsolete social system.[8]

9. Is the Law of Value Outdated?

Identification of value as the central axis for critical analysis of the economy of capitalism and thus of its presence, concealed by the workings of its transformation into observed prices, is not without its problems. Marx's own discussions of these questions invite Marxists not to limit themselves to exegeses of those texts but to dare to go further: in particular concerning (i) concrete labors of diverse character and their reduction to the concept of abstract labor; (ii) the time required for the production, circulation, and realization of surplus-value and, consequently, the relationship between living labor and transferred dead labor; (iii) the identification of use-values; (iv) the treatment of natural resources, whether privately owned or not; (v) the appropriate definition, specific to capitalism, of social labor, and the analysis of its relationship to other forms of labor; and (vi) making clear the forms of absorption of surplus-value by Department III.

The evolution of capitalism since Marx's day and the gigantic transformations that it has produced challenge Marxist analysis. A perspective that tries to stay critical and even to deepen this radical critique of capitalism requires going far beyond Marx's answers to the challenges concerning these questions. Certain Marxists, myself included, are trying to face these challenges.[9]

The current climate of opinion does not favor pursuit of these attempts to enrich Marxism, itself conceived as unbounded in its fundamental critique of the reality of the capitalist world. Instead and in place of enriching Marxist thought, one would rather prefer to bury it and claim to start over from zero. One is then usually the prisoner—whether aware of it or not—of vulgar thought, uncritical by nature. The radical critique of the reduction of the concept of progress to increasing GDP that I have put forward and—in counterpoint—the thesis that I have adopted, likening progress to emancipation, are registered here against the current climate of opinion.[10]

Current fashion is to say that the law of value is "outmoded." It would have applied to the industrial manufacturing phase of capitalism, itself made out of date by the formation of contemporary "cognitive capitalism." Forgotten is that by its essential nature capitalism, today as yesterday, is based on social relationships securing the domination of capital and the exploitation of the labor force associated with it.

The invention of the "cognitive capitalism" concept rests on a capitulation to the method of vulgar economics based on "measurement" of the specific productivities *of* "factors of production" (labor, capital, and nature). One "discovers" then that the rates of growth recorded by these partial productivities explain only 50 or 60 or 70 percent of the "general progress" (of "growth"). This difference is ascribed to the intervention of science and technology, considered as constituting a fourth, independent, "factor." Some think to have rediscovered in this "factor" the *general intellect*, whose central position in the definition of the productivity of social labor had already been pointed out by Marx. But in fact there is nothing very new there, in the sense that labor and scientific/technical knowledge have been inseparable through all the stages of human history.[11]

There is but a single productivity, that of social labor working with adequate tools, in a given natural framework, and on the basis of scientific and technical knowledge whose elements are indissociable one from the other. What vulgar economics artificially pulls apart Marx unites, thus giving the concept of value that emerges from this unity its fundamental status: the condition in its turn for a radical critique of capitalist reality.

Cognitive capitalism is an *oxymoron*. We will be able to talk of a "cognitive economy" only then, when social relations different from those on which capitalism is based have been established. Instead and in place of this deviant notion inspired by the climate of opinion, I have tried to formulate the metamorphoses that the transformations of capitalism engender in forms of expression of the law of value.

In my work I have imagined a capitalism that has reached the furthest limits of its tendency to reduce the amount of labor used for material production (*hard goods*: manufactured objects and food products) through an imaginary generalization of automation.[12] The departments of production no longer set in motion more than a tiny fraction of the labor force: what is used partly for the production of science and technology (*soft goods*) needed for that of *hard goods* and partly for services linked to consumption. In those conditions, the domination of capital is expressed in the unequal distribution of the total income, and value has no longer any meaning except on this integrated and global scale. The concept of value would persist only because society would still be alienated, mired in scarcity thinking.

Would a system that had reached such a stage of its evolution still merit the appellation "capitalism"? It would probably not. It would be a *neo-tributary* system based on systematic application of the political violence (linked to ideological procedures capable of giving it the appearance of legitimacy) indispensable for the perpetuation of inequality. Such a system is, alas, thinkable on a globalized scale: it is already in the course of being built. I have called it "apartheid on the world scale." The logic of the forces governing capitalist reproduction works in that direction, which is to say, in the direction of making "another possible world," one even more barbaric than any of the class societies that have succeeded each other throughout history.

An Algebraic Model of Extended Reproduction

1. Parameters of the System

I shall begin with a broad analysis of the system, linking real wages (and surplus-value rates) with the development rates of the productive forces. Each Department (I for production of means of production E and II for production of consumer goods C) is defined, for each phase, by an equation in value terms, as follows:

Phase 1	Department 1	$1e + ah = pe_1$
	Department 2	$1e + bh = qc_2$
Phase 2	Department 1	$1e + a\delta h = pe_1$
	Department 2	$1e + b\rho h = qc_2$
Phase 3	Department 1	$1e + a\delta^2 h = pe_1$
	Department 2	$1e + b\rho^2 h = qc_2$, etc.

The first term of each equation stands for the value of constant capital consumed in the production process, reduced to a physical unit of equipment E, estimated at the unit value e $(e_1 \neq e_2 \neq e_3,$ etc.) The second term represents the physical quantity a, b, $a\delta$, $b\rho$, etc., of total direct labor (necessary labor and surplus labor) employed by one unit of E in each Department and each phase. The parameter h measures the value product of one hour of labor (not to be confused with hourly wage). The physical product of each department, p and q respectively, is estimated at its unit value e and c (similarly $c_1 \neq c_2 \neq c_3,$ etc.).

The system comprises three pairs of parameters $(a, b, p, q, \delta,$ and $\rho)$ and two unknowns $(e$ and $c)$ for each pair of equations that describe one phase. Parameters a and b measure the physical labor intensity in the productive process (their reciprocals are related to the organic compositions), parameters p and q represent the physical product of the productive processes using one unit of equipment E in each Department, and parameter t.

Obviously δ and ρ are less than 1 since technical progress enables us to obtain, with less direct labor, a higher physical product per unit of equipment.

2. DETERMINATION OF UNIT PRICES E AND C

If we assume $h = 1$, the equations supply the pairs e and c:

$$e_1 = \frac{a}{p-1} \qquad \frac{c_1 = a + b(p-1)}{q(p-1)}$$

$$e_2 = \frac{a\delta}{p-1} \qquad \frac{c_2 = a\delta + b\rho(p-1)}{q(p-1)}$$

$$e_3 = \frac{a\delta^2}{p-1} \qquad \frac{c_3 = a\delta^2 + b\rho^2(p-1)}{q(p-1)}$$

etc.

As the first set of equations shows, as we produce the capital equipment from capital equipment and direct labor, the unit prices of e fall from one phase to the next at the rate of growth of productivity in Department I. On the other hand, consumer goods being produced from capital equipment and direct labor, the unit prices c fall at a rate that is a combination of δ and ρ.

3. EQUATIONS OF EXTENDED REPRODUCTION

If the capital equipment E is distributed between Departments I and II in the ratios n_1 and $1-n_1$, for phase 1, n_2 and $1-n_2$ for the next phase, the equations for the production in value terms are as follows:

Phase 1

D I $n_1e_1 + n_1aS_1 + n_1a(K - S_1) = n_1pe_1$

D II $(1 - n_1)e_1 + (1 - n_1)bS_1 + (1 - n_1)b(K - S_1) = (1 - n_1)qc_1$

Phase 2

D I $n_2e_2 + n_2aS_2\delta + n_2a(K - S_2)\delta = n_2pe_2$

D II $(1 - n_2)e_2 + (1 - n_2)bS_2\rho + (1 - n_2)b(K - S_2)\rho = (1 - n_2)qc_2$

K is a neutral factor of proportionality.

The dynamic equilibrium of the extended reproduction requires that two conditions be fulfilled:

1. that the wages distributed for each phase (in both Departments) enable the entire output of consumer goods produced during that phase to be bought;

2. that the surplus-value generated during one phase (in both Departments) makes it possible to purchase the entire output of Department I during the next phase.

(a) Equations of supply/demand of consumer goods:

Phase 1 $n_1aS_1 + (1-n_1)bS_1 = (1-n_1)qc_1$

Phase 2 $n_2a\delta S_2 + (1-n_2)b\rho S_2 = (1-n_2)qc_2$

(b) Equations of supply/demand of equipment:

Phase 1 $n_1pe_1 = e_2$

Phase 2 $n_2pe_2 = e_3$

Nominal Wages S are determined as follows:

$$S_1 = \frac{(1-n)\,[a+b(p-1)]}{(p-1)[an+b(1-n)]}$$

$$S_2 = \frac{(1-n)[a\delta + b\rho(p-1)]}{(p-1)[a\delta n + b\rho(1-n)]}$$

And Real Wages $S'_1 = S_1/c_1$ and $S'_2 = S_2/c_2$ are:

$$S'_1 = \frac{(1-n)q}{an + b(1-n)}$$

$$S'_2 = \frac{(1-n)q}{a\delta n + b\rho(1-n)}$$

$S'_2 > S'_1$ since the numerator remains unchanged while the denominator decreases from Phase 1 to Phase 2.

4. NUMERICAL EXAMPLES

Case	1	2	3	4	5	6
Parameters						
a	4	4	4	4	4	4
b	4	8	4	4	4	4
p	3	3	5	5	30	3
q	6	10	6	6	1	6
δ	0.5	0.5	0.5	0.5	1	0.50
ρ	0.5	0.5	0.75	0.75	0.5	1
Prices						
e_1	2	2	1	1	0.14	2
e_2	1	1	0.75	0.5	0.14	1
c_1	1	1	0.83	.83	4.14	1
c_2	0.5	0.5	0.46	0.58	2.14	0.83
Proportion						
n	0.17	0.17	0.15	0.03	0.03	0.17
Nominal Wages						
S_1	1.25	1.14	1.06	1	1	1.21
S_2	1.25	1.14	1.09	1	1	1.14
Real Wages						
S'_1	1.25	1.14	1.28	0.24	0.24	1.45
S'_2	2.50	2.28	2.37	0.47	0.47	1.96

Case 1: Equal organic compositions, equal improvement in productivity in the two Departments.

Case 2: Unequal organic compositions, equal improvement in productivity in the two Departments.

Case 3: Equal organic compositions, unequal improvement in productivity (here $\delta > \rho$).

Case 4:   The reverse assumption to the preceding case $(\delta < \rho)$.

Case 5:   Case 3 tending to be limiting, improvement in productivity being confined to Department I $(\rho = 1/2$ while $\delta = 1)$.

Case 6:   Limiting case of 4—improvement in productivity is confined to Department II $(\delta = 1/2$ while $\rho = 1)$.

CHAPTER TWO

Interest, Money, and the State

1.

In Volume III of *Capital* we find that Marx's language undergoes a sudden change. It is no longer a question of commodity fetishism and alienation, or of the value of labor-power and surplus-value. Marx speaks to us now of social classes as they appear in concrete reality—of workers, industrial capitalists, moneylenders, landowners, peasants, and so on—just as he speaks to us of incomes as they can be perceived directly, through statistics—such as wages, the industrialist's and the merchant's profit, the rate of interest, ground-rent, and so on. It is the moment when he begins to go beyond political economy and to develop his argument in terms of historical materialism.

2.

What Marx has to say about money and interest is scattered through various parts of his work. In the drafts for *Capital* (espe-

cially the *Grundrisse*) Marx gives us a series of reflections that are
as concrete as can be: observations on the policy regarding discount rates followed by the Bank of England or the Banque de
France at particular moments of history, critical thoughts relating to the commentaries of the principal economists of the time
on these policies, and so on. No explicit theory is expounded in
Volume III, however. Marx puts before us a theory of the rate of
interest that runs like this: (a) interest is the reward of money
capital (not of productive capital); (b) it is therefore a category
of distribution; (c) the rate of interest is determined by the inter-
play of supply and demand for money capital, in which two subclasses, lenders and borrowers, confront each other; and (d) this
rate is indeterminate and can be situated at any point between a
floor (zero interest) and a ceiling (a rate of interest equal to the
rate of profit).

This theory seems to me inadequate. Indeed, Marx does not
show any particular fondness for resorting to "supply and
demand," and when he does so he usually raises at the outset the
question: what real forces determine this supply and this
demand? Here, however, we find nothing of the sort. The theory
is inadequate, in the first place, because the floor and the ceiling
in question are too low and too high, respectively. The rate of
interest cannot be zero because, if it were, there would be no
lenders. It cannot be equal to the rate of profit, for then the productive capitalists would cease to produce, and so they would
not borrow.

Above all, however, it is inadequate because the resort to pos-
tulating two subclasses of capitalists, imagined as being independent of each other, contradicts Marx's thesis on money. Marx considers the demand for money, the social need for a certain quantity of money, as being determined *a priori* by the conditions of
expanded reproduction, with lines of production and prices
determined independently of the quantity of money available.
This rigorously anti-quantitativist position has not only been

accepted by all Marxists, it has morover been continued and made more precise in relation to the schemata of expanded reproduction (see chapter one). It suggests, moreover, that the supply of money adjusts itself to this need, this demand. The creation and destruction of credit by the banking system fulfills this function.

If that is the case, one cannot see how the confrontation of supply and demand could in any way determine the rate of interest. We do not observe two independent subclasses meeting in a market for lending and borrowing. What we do observe is, on the one hand, those who demand—namely the productive capitalists as a whole, their demand being dependent on the extent to which their own capital is insufficient—and, on the other hand, institutions that respond to their demand. What do these institutions represent? They do not represent a subclass, that of the bankers. Even if the banks are private establishments, and even if the bank of issue to which they are subject, since it is the ultimate lender, is also a private establishment, state policy has always intervened (even in the nineteenth century) to regulate this supply of money. The monetary system of capitalism has always been relatively centralized. The point is that the bank, like the state, represents the collective interest of the bourgeois class. The "two hundred families" who held shares in the Banque de France were not merely money-lending capitalists; they also constituted, through this bank, the principal nucleus of the French bourgeoisie. Thus, we have here a contrast not between two subclasses but between the capitalists as individuals in rivalry with one another (the fragmentation of capital) and the capitalist class organized collectively. The state and the monetary institutions are not the expression of particular interests counterposed to other particular interests, but of the collective interests of the class, the means whereby confrontation among separate interests is regulated.

3.

The radical critique of political economy initiated by Marx grasped right away the reality of the "real economy/financial image" duality proper to capitalism. Capitalism is not expressed solely through private property in the real means of production (factories, inventories, and other such things). It is equally expressed through ownership instruments relative to these "real" properties. The joint-stock-company offers the classical example of the mode of financialization associated with the circulation as commodities of these ownership instruments. The real capital/fictitious capital duality is thus not the result of a "deviation," still less of a "recent deviation." Through it, even at the beginning, was made manifest the alienation specific to the capitalist mode of production. That alienation puts in the place of the productivity of social labor—the only objective reality—the productivity of separate "factors" of production among which, of course, is capital, assimilated to ownership instruments.

This association of the two faces—real and "fictitious"—of accumulation is begun in Volume III, but Marx intended to develop the discussion of this question in the following volumes, which he did not live long enough to write.

The alienation of the modern capitalist world, like that of earlier epochs, separates "soul from body" and assigns to the soul (today, property) predominance over the body (today, labor). Our modern left, alas, prisoner of empiricist positivism (in particular the Anglo-Saxon variety) and simultaneously allergic to Marx, is by that very fact ill-equipped to grasp the immanence of this duality and of unavoidable financialization.

Financialization is thus in no way a regrettable deviation, and its explosive growth does not operate to the detriment of growth in the "real" productive economy. There is a whole lot of ingenuousness to propositions in the style of "social democracy taken seriously" that suggest controlling financial expansion and mobilizing the "financial surplus" to support "real growth." The tendency to stagnate is inherent in the monopoly capitalism superbly analyzed by Sweezy, Baran, and Magdoff. Financialization then provides not only the sole possible outlet for surplus capital, it also provides the sole stimulus to the slack growth observed, since the 1970s, in the United States, Europe, and Japan. To roll back financialization would thus merely weaken yet further the growth of the "real" economy. Simultaneously, this inescapable financialization increases the fragility of the global equilibrium and multiplies the instances of "financial crises" which, in turn, are transmitted to the real economy. Monopoly capitalism is of necessity financialized; its reproduction goes from "bubble" to "bubble." A first bubble necessarily bursts as soon as the pursuit of "unlimited" growth is hampered for any reason; and the system can get out of the financial crisis occasioned by this bursting only by fabricating and inflating a new bubble.

Analysts from the "critical left" (those unwilling to sign up openly to social liberalism) believe themselves able to propose policies capable of "regulating" capitalism and forcing it to take into consideration the legitimate social demands of workers and citizens. They fear being called "unrealistic radicals" (or even "Marxists"!) were they to come up with anything more. But it is their propositions that are completely unrealistic, for reasons given by Baran, Sweezy, and Magdoff in their precocious analyses of "financialization," which they grasped at its very beginning in the 1980s.

The financial collapse of 2008 has occasioned a flood of disinformation, organized by the dominant media with the help of "experts," accusing the banks of having "abused deregulation," of having "made errors of judgment" (subprime mortgages), even of dishonesty—thus distinguishing and whitewashing the "good capitalists" who are innovators and who invest in real production. Such dissociation is meaningless; the same oligopolies dominate quite equally places of production and financial institutions. Even worse, this dissociation proceeds from a "theory" that knows not that a class state can function, precisely as a class state, only by placing itself above the interests of particular parcels of capital so that—especially through finances—the collective interests of capital should prevail. "Regulation" is the name given to this permanent and unavoidable state intervention.

This regulation takes place in two domains where the collective interest of the class has predominance. The first is regulation of the trade cycle and the second is regulation of international competition.

4.

Regulation of the conjunction does not signify suppression of the cycle but, on the contrary, an ordered intensification of its scope, as a means whereby to maximize the pace of accumulation in time of prosperity and then to control this through liquidations, restructurings, and concentrations in times of crisis. This form of regulation is given ideological expression in the monetarist theories of the conjuncture—that is, in the attempt to rationalize the bourgeois practice of competition. The rate of interest appears as the supreme instrument for this regulation.

When the state acts through the monetary system to impose an increase in the rate of interest, the central authority is intervening actively in economic life in the collective interest of capital. The raising of the rate of interest intensifies the crisis, multiplying bankruptcies. But it thereby accelerates the process of concentration of capital, the condition for the modernizing of the apparatus of production and the conversions that have become necessary. Contrariwise, the reduction in the rate of interest accelerates the growth rate and enables the economy in question to derive maximum benefit from its restored external competitiveness.

5.

The second domain is that of competition among national capitalisms. In the nineteenth century, in Marx's time, the rule of the game where international competition among the central capitalist formations was concerned was that of the gold standard (dual convertibility, internal and external). The flow this way and that of the yellow metal therefore responded to the differences among interest rates. This flow constituted a source, positive or negative, of the supply of money at the disposal of the national monetary institutions. The practicing of monetary policies—that is, the manipulation of rates of interest—was therefore a means of intervening in the conduct of relations among the different national formations. Here, too, increasing the rate of interest in times of crisis helped to reestablish the external equilibrium when this was threatened during the conversion period, by attracting into the country "floating" capital from abroad.

The methods of managing international competition are no longer those known and criticized by Marx. The abandonment of the gold standard and the generalization of flexible exchange rates on the one hand, and the puffing up of the Department III for the absorption of excess surplus-value, on the other, have simultaneously imposed and allowed extreme diversity in economic and financial policy methods. These interventions are based on a healthy dose of empiricism: there is "what has worked" and what has not. But they likewise deploy a vast repertory of "theories," ranging from Keynes to Hayek and on to Chicago monetarism. They continually reformulate models that claim to integrate the "givens" provided by observation and, consequently, to guarantee the efficacious working of the policies envisaged on that basis. To extend the critique that Marx began of the bases and methods of vulgar economics requires, in turn, the critique of all these post-Marxian theories emerging from the field of vulgar economics.[1]

Naturally, study of the domain of international competition cannot be reduced to abstract analysis of the mechanical relations linking different economic magnitudes, national and foreign: the volume and price of imports and exports, the flow of capital and its response to the rates of profit and of interest, and so on. In this domain it is always possible to claim that one can derive economic laws from empirical observation of the facts. Thousands of econometric models have been constructed with this end in view, but the results obtained from them have proved meager. In most cases, the laws inferred from observation of the past cannot be confirmed in the future and do not endow the public authorities with effective instruments of control. The reason for this is that what is essential often lies outside these models: the rate of progress of the productive forces, the results of the class struggle, and the effects of the latter upon the former.

It is my opinion that the reason why Marx did not construct an economic theory of international relations is to be sought here. As we know, Marx did say, in the *Grundrisse* and in several other preliminary sketches for *Capital*, that there would be a chapter on international relations, but he never wrote such a chapter. Was this because he did not have the time? I think, rather, that he gave up his intention because he realized that no economic theory of world trade was possible. Before tackling the economic aspect of international relations (the "economic appearances," the visible part of the iceberg), it was necessary to carry out a thorough analysis in the terms of historical materialism. Just as an analysis of the class struggle on the scale of the national formations had provided the basis for the theory of the capitalist mode, so an analysis of the class struggle on the scale of the world capitalist system is a prerequisite for an analysis of the world economy. But an "economic" theory of international relations is impossible.[2] After rejecting the economic theories of adjustment of the balance of payments, I myself decided in favor of a line of research directed at the class struggles on a world scale, which shape the structural adjustments among national formations within the framework of which the apparent economic laws operate. I had occasion to come back to the problem when I examined the questions of historical materialism and their relation to the law of value operating on the scale of worldwide accumulation.[3]

6.

The two domains—the internal conjuncture and external competitive capacity—are closely linked. This is why the instrument of monetary policy is still the instrument *par excellence* of the economic policy of the bourgeois state.

Here, then, are two domains in which forces are at work that determine the rate of interest: two domains that belong to the realm of historical materialism, not of economics. Economic theory (meaning *pure* economic theory—that is, a science independent of historical materialism) ignores the state, the collective expression of the bourgeoisie, and the national states of the central bourgeoisies that are in conflict with one another. But Marxism never fails to take into account these aspects of social reality, and never deals with them in isolation from an economy that is supposed to ignore them.[4]

Bourgeois economistic ideology has produced, in this domain, dozens of theories, thousands of models, and as many recipes and schools of thought. But the characteristic feature of all these theories, and the reason they remain ideological, is that they avoid the role played by crisis in the restoration of order (because one must not cast doubt on the harmonious character of capitalist growth, crisis has always to be presented as something accidental) and also the nature of the struggle over shares in domination of the world (because bourgeois ideology counterposes economics, where peaceful competition is supposed to reign, to politics, which is admitted to be the scene of evil aggressive behavior).

Undoubtedly, too, the precise content of these theories has had to be adapted, more or less, to the actual evolution of the system. The changes in the predominant forms of competition (the formation of monopolies), the interpenetration of industrial and financial capital, the disappearance of internal convertibility into precious metals, the organization of international monetary blocs—all these phenomena, which figure in the analysis of imperialism, have modified the rules of the money game and the relations between the internal and international conjunctures.

It remains true that the supreme purpose of this economistic ideology is to construct a general model of monetary equilibrium, completing the model of real equilibrium as constructed by Walras.

The method of historical materialism is the very opposite of that which is promoted by research directed toward general monetary equilibrium. This is so, not because it ignores monetary techniques and policies, but because it goes further, placing these techniques and policies in their setting, as instruments of the bourgeois state in the internal and international class struggle.

CHAPTER THREE

Ground Rent

1.

We know that Marx took over Ricardo's theory of differential rent. This was not an example of "marginalist" reasoning. Marginalism assumes that production varies through the association of increasing doses of one factor with another factor, whose quantity is fixed. Here, the same dose of total social labor (with the same proportion of direct and indirect labor) gives different results depending on the quality of the soil (which, not being homogeneous, is therefore not a factor). Marx, too, as we know, developed the theory of differential rent in the same spirit, by introducing an intensive "Rent II" to complement the extensive "Rent I." By doing so he showed himself to be aware that fertility is not something natural, but results from the labor invested in what may be called "the production of soil"—a fact well known to agronomists and to everyone familiar with country life, but continually overlooked by economists both classical and neoclassical.

It is hard to deny that differential rents exist. But the explanation that they are determined by the difference between the productivity of labor on a given plot of land and the productivity of labor on the worst plot has not always carried conviction. An author who claims to be Marxist, Henri Regnault, has tried to build a theory of rent based upon the determination of agricultural prices by average conditions of production, just as in industry.[1] The good-quality plot of land thus receives a positive differential rent, while the poor-quality one (poor in relation to the "average" plot) receives a negative differential rent. The latter is possible only if it comes as a deduction from an absolute rent that is greater in amount. Differential rents are thus presented as resulting from transfers made from the owners of worse plots to the owners of better plots. On this basis Regnault proposes a reconsideration of the analysis of "external economies."

This is certainly a stimulating reflection. But what is truly the point of Marx's argument (and Ricardo's)? What worries Regnault is that, as he sees it, this argument brings in "demand" in a way that is unusual with Marx. I do not agree. I think that the argument is based on different grounds—namely, on whether or not the average conditions are reproducible. If the average conditions are indeed reproducible (crystallized in equipment that can always be acquired) then the capitalists receive super-profits— and not rents (not even monopoly rents)—that are positive or negative depending on whether they use equipment that is superior or inferior to the average. But if we are dealing with the natural conditions of production, that is, by definition, with conditions that are *not* reproducible (over and above the degree to which they may be modified, as envisaged in Rent II), does not the concept of an "average" vanish?

However that may be, whether we are concerned with industry (reproducible means) or with agriculture (non-reproducible conditions), demand enters into the matter in both cases, and in the same way. When a productive system is given (and it matters little here whether it be expressed in values, as with Marx, or in prices, as with Ricardo and Sraffa), this presupposes that production be adequately adjusted to demand: the quantitative distribution of the production in excess of productive consumption needed between each product $1. \ldots, i \ldots, n$, corresponds to an equivalent distribution of demand between wage-earners and capitalists (including in this the demand resulting from expanded reproduction). Marx does not eliminate use-value and does not fall into a way of looking at things that is based one-sidedly upon exchange-value.

2.

However, what interests us here is absolute rent, that which is paid for the worst land (*not* marginal land). Marx relates the existence of such rent to that of a class: the landowners.

Is the level of this rent determined? If so, why and how? Marx might have used an argument here similar to his argument about interest, saying that absolute rent is indeterminate and results from the confrontation of two classes, the landlords and the capitalists, with merely a floor—zero—and a ceiling—a level of absolute rent that absorbs all the surplus-value.

Why not? For we know that rent is a category of distribution, since the landowner plays no part in the process of production. Obviously, each of these two forms of transfer income has its own status: if the landowners were to refuse to lease their land then no production could take place whereas, if money were to disappear, it would be re-created. The soil forms part of the *natural* conditions of production; money is one of its *social* conditions.

Apart from that, though, the same argument could be advanced. It would incur the same criticism, namely that the floor is too low (with zero rent the land would no longer be made available for renting) and the ceiling too high (if rent absorbed the whole of surplus-value the capitalists would stop producing).

The question seems to be, then: is rent determined by some economic law that forms part of the whole system of laws governing price formation, or by a pure and simple relation of power? Actually, this question is badly put and needs to be replaced by another: how does this class struggle (between landowners and capitalists) operate on a given economic basis and how does it modify that basis? Only thus will the two domains, that of economics and that of the class struggle, not be separated but be taken together, so defining here, as elsewhere, the true domain of social science: historical materialism.

Yet Marx here gives a simple answer to the question of how rent is determined, one that refers to economic reality only. He affirms that it is the difference in the organic composition of capital, which is lower in agriculture, that determines the value retained by the landowner. I have already said that I find this proposition unacceptable,[2] both on the empirical plane (is the organic composition in agriculture always lower? why so? and if it were *higher* should the rent be negative?) and on the plane of logic. As regards the latter, even if the organic composition were higher in agriculture, could not the rent imposed by landownership act so as to distort prices (as compared to prices of production without rent) just as competition among capitalists distorts prices of production (as compared with values)? In that case, though, are we slipping into indeterminacy?

3.

So far as I know, only one writer, Regnault, attempting to substitute a different economic determination for that offered by Marx, has tried to link rent with the rate of interest. This is his key argument presented in the form of an imaginary discourse: "You own the capital, I own the land. You can take a lease of my land, while I can borrow your capital, in return for paying the rate of interest.

If you invest 100, you will gain 100r (r being the rate of profit). If I borrow 100, I gain 100$(r - i)$. For the lease of my land I require you to pay me 100$(r - i)$."

Regnault concludes that absolute rent results from the existence of a capital market wherein the rate of interest is lower than the average rate of profit. He also notes that this determination must not be confused with the determination of the price of land by capitalizing the rent.

What worries me here is that the capitalist who agreed to pay a rent equal to 100$(r - i)$ would no longer be making the average profit r. Why, then, should he choose to invest in this branch, if he cannot add the average profit to his costs of production? Why would he agree to give up his status as a capitalist (receiving r) and be satisfied with that of a money-lender, receiving $r - (r - i)$, that is, i? Though the problem has been shifted back, it is still there.

4.

Most Marxists who have concerned themselves with the question of rent—among those who are not content merely to expound what Marx wrote—have inclined toward indeterminacy on the economic plane, after rejecting determination by comparative organic composition. All we can deduce from a Ricardian, neo-Ricardian, or Sraffian system into which absolute rent has been introduced (which Ricardo refused to do, but which, as we have seen from Marx, can be done) is that rent and profit are inverse functions one of the other. Economic theory cannot explain the *level* of this rent—cannot tell us what determines it.

It seems, indeed, undeniable that the levy upon the net product constituted by absolute rent modifies relative prices and reduces the rate of profit just as an increase in wages does. (We know that relative prices and the rate of profit depend on the level of wages.) This fact can be proven by using either Marx's transformation schemata or a Sraffian model.

Let us take, for example, a transformation schema with two branches, (1) and (2), a rate of surplus-value of 100 percent, and different organic compositions. Without absolute rent, the transformation schema, in the case of the illustrative example set out in the table below, gives a rate of profit of 28.5 percent and prices p_1 = 38.5 and p_2 = 51.5.

SURPLUS PRODUCT

	Constant capital	Variable capital	Form surplus value	Form Profit	Values	Prices of Production
	(1)	(2)	(3)	(4)	(5)	(6)
Branch (1)	20	10	10	8.5	40	38.5
Branch (2)	30	10	10	11.5	50	51.5
Total	50	20	20	20	90	90

If, now, we assume that branch (1) has to bear an absolute rent of 4 (in value $\rho = 4$) for an average rate of profit proportional to capital advanced (30 and 40, respectively) we have:

Branch (1) $\quad p_1 = 30(1+r) + 4(\rho = 4)$

Branch (2) $\quad p_2 = 40(1+r)$

and: $\quad p_1 + p_2 = 90$

which gives: $\quad p_1 = 40.9, p_2 = 49.1,$ and $r = 23$ percent

There is, of course, no reason why the levy represented by absolute rent should be determined in advance and in value terms. All that can be said is that, if it exists ($\rho \neq 0$), then, on the one hand, it entails a modification of relative prices and of the average rate of profit, and, on the other hand, its magnitude could be determined in real terms, like wages, as a function of the prices themselves, in the general form:

$$\rho = ap_1 + \beta p_2$$

It is also possible, of course, to include rent in a Sraffian schema and arrive at the same conclusions. Absolute rent expresses a social relation and cannot be determined by a simple, natural, economic law.

It seems to me, however, precisely for that reason that this critique stops just at the point where the problems start to become interesting. What I see as important is how rent is determined in the domain of historical materialism—for it is indeed determined in that domain.

Historical materialism, as has been said, cannot be reduced to a games theory detached from its economic basis. It is not a formal exercise enabling us to decide the point of equilibrium between two or among three partners (bourgeoisie and proletariat, or these two classes plus the landowners) who are in rivalry over the sharing of a given cake.

5.

Before turning to this analysis, however, I think it is relevant to recall that Marx already replied to this problematic in his own way, both in *Capital* and in some other, "political," writings.

After determining rent by comparative organic composition, Marx moves on and in the chapters that follow examines the history of rent. What does he do then? He forgets all about organic compositions, makes no further allusion to them, does not even try to give any indication of what they are. Moreover, he stops talking about landowners in general and speaks instead, when he is dealing with England, of "landlords," whom he counterposes to "farmers," and, when he is dealing with France, of "peasants." Here we enter right into the realm of historical materialism.

The case that Marx studies, that of England, is rich in lessons concerning his method, the way he determines rent in the realm of historical materialism. So long as the class of landlords shared power with the bourgeoisie in England (and here we see once more the state intervening in order to widen the "economic" domain), a high rent cut off part of profit. This rent was determined by the division of labor between agriculture and industry, which had to be maintained so long as the English economy was obliged to feed its workers without importing cereals (this being practically forbidden by the Corn Laws). It can be shown that, in order to meet the requirement of equilibrium of supply and demand for agricultural products, on the one hand, and industrial products, on the other, the economic system assigned a given level to rent. If it rose above that level, accumulation in industry would be slowed down and then the supply of grain would be greater than the demand. If it fell below that level, the opposite process would ensue.

This example shows that Marx did not exclude the structure of demand from his analysis, though he did not reduce this analysis to a "general equilibrium" à la Walras, which is merely a static description and—as an explanation—mere tautology. Marx transcends the problem by envisaging dynamic equilibrium. Rent, determined immediately by a confrontation between classes, operates on the basis of economic laws, of an economic reality in which equilibrium of supply and demand is inescapable.

We have seen how Marx integrates demand into the process of accumulation, and how the dynamic equilibrium of supply and demand for production goods and consumer goods is what closes the system, determining at one and the same time, on the basis of a given real wage (the value of labor-power), the relative prices and the rate of profit. This first model comprised only two classes (proletarians and capitalists) and two forms of income (wages and profits). The closing of the system implied a certain distribution of labor-power between Departments I and II—that is, an adequate mode of division of labor, in conformity with the structure of demand.

Let us continue this same line of reasoning, after introducing absolute rent $\rho = f(p_1 p_2 \ldots)$. If the technical data of production (material inputs and inputs of direct labor) and the real wage (the value of labor-power) are given, and if we know also what the rent is spent on (say, for instance, it is wholly spent on luxury goods), then for a given system there is only one level of rent that makes dynamic equilibrium possible. The position is the same, *mutatis mutandis*, as with wages. If the rent rises any higher than that level, then profit is reduced and growth slows, affecting the labor market so as to reduce wages. Conversely, if the rent falls below that level, this entails a crisis of realization: excessive profits foster an increase in production that cannot find an outlet, if the level of wages remains unchanged.

The model includes thenceforth three classes and three types of income. The struggles and alliances among these three classes operate on the basis of an economic system that is defined by adequate modes of the division of labor, and in their turn, as we have seen, where two fundamental classes are concerned, these struggles and alliances modify the conditions in which the system functions.

The class struggles do modify this economic basis. How, in fact, did the English bourgeoisie succeed in reducing the rent charged by the landlords? By abolishing the Corn Laws and substituting for English wheat American wheat, which paid no rent (since there were no landlords on the other side of the Atlantic). It was thus by establishing a new alliance of classes, between English capitalists and American farmers, that the English bourgeoisie freed itself from its local adversary. In its turn, this redistribution of forces modified the division of labor. In England it made possible accelerated industrialization, and in America accelerated development of agriculture. On the scale of the entity "England-America," the economic laws of equilibrium between supply and demand reappear—"without rent."

When, in contrast to this case, Marx analyzes the case of France, he starts from the alliance between the bourgeoisie and the peasants. Here, there were peasants, who owned their land and their equipment and exploited wage-labor only marginally. Marx refrains from splitting the peasant into three beings—the landowner, the capitalist, and the proletarian—in the way that our neoclassical economists later presumed to do. Marx knows that what is involved here is a peasant mode of production articulated with and dominated by the capitalist mode. He knows that, in this peasant mode, production for subsistence remains important, but also that domination by capital compels the marketing of part of the product. The alliance between the bourgeoisie and the peasants (an unequal alliance, in which the bourgeoisie was in command, but an alliance nonetheless, directed against the proletariat) found expression in the agricultural policy of the French state (protectionism and other measures permitting agricultural products to be sold at a relatively high price). It may be that this policy resulted in the peasants' standard of living being higher than that of the proletarians—the comparison is difficult to make. But it is pointless to give the name of "rent" to the difference between the total income of the peasants (their subsistence plus what they got for the produce they marketed) and the sum of the counterpart of their labor and the reward of their capital. Here again, this alliance had "economic" effects, and it functioned on the basis of a division of labor that was different from the division prevailing in England.

Gradually, as the proletarian danger retreated (after 1871, and with imperialist expansion) the bourgeoisie attached less importance to its alliance with the peasantry. It took steps to reduce agricultural prices and ended, though belatedly, by aligning the reward of peasant labor with the value of labor-power. The stress laid by an entire line of research in France upon the "formal domination"[3] that deprived peasant proprietorship of its content (since this proprietorship no longer conferred the right to a pseudo-rent) finds here the objective conditions that have enabled it to develop systematically. Colonial settlement, and the social-democratic hegemony over the proletariat that accompanied it, facilitated this evolution. Settlement in Algeria benefited from the availability of "lands without owners" (owing to the laws expropriating the Algerians) and Algerian wine, which paid no rent, made it possible to lower the income of French winegrowers.

6.

This line of analysis of rent alone seems to me to be capable of placing the problem of the determination of rent correctly in the realm of historical materialism.

From this point of view, the French school—before it gave up on Marxism—brought some very fine contributions to the analysis of the submission of the "independent" peasantry to dominant capital. It also, into the bargain, dealt analytically with "urban ground rent" in analogous terms, thereby enriching Marx.

As for our contribution, we refer the reader to our previous writings.[4] This contribution, concerned above all with the linkage/domination between the capitalism of the imperialist epoch and the peasant modes of the periphery, represents thus a transition to the continuation of our discourse, which takes as its objective putting the method of historical materialism to work as an instrument of analysis, no longer of the capitalist mode (and of the central formations) but now of the global capitalist system (the central and peripheral formations in their mutual relationship).

CHAPTER FOUR

Accumulation on a Global Scale and Imperialist Rent

I now take up what, among the metamorphoses of value, seems to me to be—by far—the most consequential, operating in decisive fashion in all the fields of social struggle and in international and national political conflicts of the modern world. I mean *the transformation of value into globalized value.*

I had "sniffed out" the importance of this question in the course of writing my doctoral dissertation (1954–1956), even though it took me a decade to express, in a still-clumsy way, a first formulation of it. This was not a question posed by Marx. So it is in that precise sense that I will claim—without false modesty—to have contributed to extending and enriching Marxism. The thesis has scarcely been convincing to the thinkers of Western Marxisms, with the exception, as far as I know, of Paul Sweezy, Harry Magdoff, and Giovanni Arrighi. Contrariwise, it has been well received in Asia and Africa where, by diverse but finally converging paths, it has contributed to fashioning an Asian and African face of Marxism, to the emergence of a veritable "shoreless Marx."[1]

The argument is simple, though twofold.

Historical capitalism, as it has really existed, has always been imperialist in the very precise sense that the mechanisms inherent to its worldwide spread, far from progressively "homogenizing" economic conditions on a planetary scale, have, on the contrary, reproduced and deepened the contrast, counterposing the dominant (imperialist) centers to the dominated peripheries. In this asymmetry is affirmed, with violence still greater than that contemplated by Marx, the law of pauperization that is indissolubly linked to the logic of capital accumulation.

Still, despite this permanent asymmetry, capitalism is one and indivisible. Capitalism is not the United States and Germany, with India and Ethiopia only "halfway" capitalist. Capitalism is the United States and India, Germany and Ethiopia, taken together. This means that labor-power has but a single value, that which is associated with the level of development of the productive forces taken globally (the *General Intellect* on that scale). In answer to the polemical argument that had been put against him—how can one compare the value of an hour of work in the Congo to that of a labor-hour in the United States?—Arghiri Emmanuel wrote: just as one compares the value of an hour's work by a New York hairdresser to that of an hour's labor by a worker in Detroit. You have to be consistent. You cannot invoke "inescapable" globalization when it suits you and refuse to consider it when you find it troublesome!

However, though there exists but one sole value of labor-power on the scale of globalized capitalism, that labor-power is nonetheless recompensed at very different rates. Certainly, variations in the price of labor-power do exist within the central capitalist countries themselves: but their amplitude is multiplied tenfold on the global scale.

We can thus model the expressions of this reality and, starting with them, measure, if we want to take the trouble, their amplitude—which is to say, the amplitude of the transfer of value from the peripheries to the centers: A transfer that is hidden behind the observed price and wage system, and as such unthinkable for vulgar empiricist economics. So I will, in the first part of this chapter, formulate the terms of the modeling needed to grasp the metamorphosis of the law of value into the law of globalized value.

The second series of arguments concerns access to natural resources, the norms governing their administration, and how they are used.

We are here no longer "in" the law of value, but at its frontiers. That is why Marx does not confound "value" with "wealth," as do all the vulgar economists, including supposed Marxists "open" to the "contributions" of conventional economics. Marx concludes his radical critique in *Capital* with the affirmation that capitalist accumulation is founded on the destruction of the bases of all wealth: human beings and their natural environment.

It took a wait lasting a century and a half until our environmentalists rediscovered that reality, now become blindingly clear. It is true that historical Marxisms had largely passed an eraser over the analyses advanced by Marx on this subject and taken the point of view of the bourgeoisie—equated to an atemporal "rational" point of view—in regard to the exploitation of natural resources. So we have to go back and take up this question from point zero. Of course, bourgeois economics was forced to take into consideration the "price" of access to those resources that could be privately owned, and so conceived an "extractive rent" ("Mining Rent") analogous in its way to ground rent. Henceforward we recognize that the challenge is on a quite different scale, which must deal in an integrated way with the totality of resources that are not to be privately owned. As we will see, vulgar economics cannot do this while the enrichment of shoreless Marxism makes it possible.

The question of the treatment of natural resources is inseparable from the analysis of asymmetric globalization resulting from capitalist expansion. For unequal access to the utilization of planetary resources constitutes in its turn the second dimension, no

less important than that following from the globalized hierar-
chization of labor-power prices and imperialist rent. So we will
take up these questions in the second part of this chapter.

1. THE GLOBAL HIERARCHY
OF THE PRICES OF LABOR POWER

The world system does not appear to lend itself to formalization
in algebraic terms. It is, in fact, made up of segments that appear
heterogeneous and even incongruous: groups of capitalist firms
producing commodities by means of more or less efficient techniques and employing wage-labor at various rates of real remuneration; zones that seem to be precapitalist, where products, not
all of which are marketed, are produced in the setting of various
peasant modes, with or without extortion of surplus labor in various forms (ground rent, tribute, and the like); groups of natural
resources (minerals), access to which is more or less obstructed,
depending on the laws of the states concerned—on whether or
not they appropriate the resources. Furthermore, no world economy can be analyzed without considering the states; these exist
not only on the plane of political reality but also on the economic
plane. The economic exchanges among these states have to balance; there are national monetary systems, some of these are
linked with others, and so on.

Any attempt at translating this set of realities into a system of
equations seems to be a long shot. Even summing up a system
regarded as being close to a pure capitalist mode in a model,
whether Marxian (with Department I and Department II
expressed in values) or Sraffian, constitutes a simplification that
must be surrounded with many precautions.

I do not think, however, that resort to relatively simple
schemata must be ruled out. Each of these schemata will possess
some value, not merely pedagogic but scientific (even though

such value is necessarily limited)—provided that we define precisely what data we are using and realize what these data signify.

Here is an example. One can define a system in which commodities $1 \ldots, i \ldots, z$ are produced, some by means of techniques characterized by material inputs A_{ij}^c and quantities of direct labor L_{ij}^c, and others by means of other techniques characterized by inputs A_{ij}^p and quantities of labor L_i^p. This system can be characterized as follows: (a) a single rate of profit r, the only regulator of distribution throughout the system; (b) a single price P^i for each product i; (c) two different wage levels W^c and W^p ($W^c > W^p$). Certain commodities (l to m) have, under these conditions, a lower price if they are produced with techniques $(A_{ij}^c L_i^c)$, others (n to z) with techniques $(A_{ij}^p L_i^p)$, it being understood that those produced according to the first formula pay the wages W^c, and the others pay the wages W^p, and that in every case the capital receives the same reward r.

This system might illustrate (without explaining) the conditions of reproduction (equilibrium between supply and demand, and so on) in a model reflecting a certain reality, namely: (a) all products are world commodities (these commodities have only one price—that which is obtained under the conditions that make it the lowest); (b) capital is mobile on the world scale; (c) labor is *not* mobile, and obtains different rewards at the center and at the periphery. In other words, it is a schematization of the way the production process has been turned into a world process in the imperialist epoch.

A model of this kind can be expressed either in Sraffian terms or in terms of value. It is not a substitute for historical materialism, any more than the schemata in Volume II of *Capital* are. But it is useful because it makes explicit what seems to be an objective economic law in such a system, and therefore a basis upon which historical materialism can operate.

If we accept the data of the system and try to stay within its framework, we are obliged at the outset to ask three questions.

First, why in the peripheral zone do they not combine the techniques $A^c_{ij}L^c_i$ with the wages W^p, which would give a higher profit than can be received with the techniques $A^p_{ij}L^p_i$? Second, why in this case doesn't all capital migrate from the center to the periphery? Third, at a given moment, the distribution of techniques being what it is, is the international division of labor that results from it (the center specializing in branches of production l to m, the periphery in n to z) compatible with equilibrium in exchange, since the fractions of products l to m exchanged for products n to z, at prices pi, ought to be equal?

Economic theory endeavors to answer these questions, and fails. I have examined the various theories produced to explain the equilibrium of the balances of payments (theories of price effects or exchange effects), have shown the circular character of these arguments (based on the quantity theory of money or on assumptions regarding elasticities of demand that presuppose the result), and have concluded that they amounted to nothing more than an expression of the ideology of universal harmonies.[2] But when economic theory, turning away from these nonsensical notions, speaks of "re-equilibrating" income effects, it hits the nail on the head. By so doing, however, it invites us to ask the real question, which sits outside its own field: how are the structures adjusted to each other—that is, by the effect of what forces does this adjustment take place? (What is involved here are class struggles on the world scale.)

The model illustrates one possible case: the case in which labor is not exploited uniformly—that is, when the rates of surplus-value are unequal. In order to introduce this hypothesis (it is, at this stage, no more than a hypothesis) we need to construct the model in terms of values, rather than directly in price terms.

Unequal exploitation is manifested in unequal exchange. Unequal exploitation (and the unequal exchange that results from it) dictates inequality in the international distribution of labor. It distorts the structure of demand, accelerating self-centered accumulation at the center while hindering dependent, extroverted accumulation in the periphery.

2. ONE ACCUMULATION MODEL, OR TWO?

I have proposed two accumulation models, one involving the center and the other the periphery.[3] The model involving the center is governed by the articulation of *Capital*'s two Departments, I and II, which, by that fact, expresses the coherence of a self-centered capitalist economy. Contrariwise, in the periphery model, the articulation that governs the reproduction of the system links exports (the motive force) to (induced) consumption. The model is "outward-turned" (as opposed to "self-centered"). It conveys a "dependence," in the sense that the periphery adjusts "unilaterally" to the dominant tendencies on the scale of the world system in which it is integrated, these tendencies being the very ones governed by the demands of accumulation at the center.

Of course, each of the models (central and peripheral) has gone through successive phases that have their own characteristics. For example, the peripheral model passes from a primary stage (export of agricultural and mineral products) to a stage of industrialization through import substitution (the general model for the second half of the twentieth century, the "Bandung era,") and then to a stage of generalized industrialization with exports competitive to the center's industries (the Chinese model of the 1990s). Nevertheless, the model remains peripheral in that it is inscribed within unilateral adjustment to the demands of globalization.

These conditions, governing accumulation on a world scale, thus reproduce unequal development. They make clear that the underdeveloped countries are so because they are super-exploited and not because they are backward (if in fact they have been retarded, that is what permitted their super-exploitation).

This view, moreover, is confirmed by experience. All projections in constant prices of dependent development policies end up with blockage by a double deficit: of the balance of payments and of the government budget; all current-price (relative prices of imports and exports) projections of those policies arrive at this same blockage even more rapidly. This fact has but one explanation: that the structure of prices is deformed (as an effect of combined class struggles on the world scale) in a way that favors aggravated exploitation of the periphery.

"Catching up," in the sense given to this expression by the false "stages of growth" theory, becomes impossible within the framework of "really existing capitalism," imperialist by its very nature. This conclusion does not apply solely to the past: it challenges the construction of the future. The idea that the so-called emerging countries have embarked on a catch-up path thanks to their deepened integration into globalization such as it is (and it cannot be otherwise) is baseless.

The "two models," nonetheless, constitute but a single reality, that of accumulation operative on a world scale, and characterized by the articulation of Marx's Departments I and II—grasped henceforward at the global scale and no longer at the scale of societies at the center.

For the periphery's exports, at this scale, become constitutive elements of constant capital and variable capital (whose prices they lower), while their imports fulfill functions analogous to those of Department III: that is to say, they facilitate the realization of excess surplus-value.

3. SOCIAL STRUGGLES AND INTERNATIONAL CONFLICTS IN A GLOBAL PERSPECTIVE

The model does not imply that the openly capitalist form of exploitation becomes general throughout the system. The system merely assumes commodity production, and that the commodities produced are world commodities. Although introducing a rate of profit r in each equation corresponding to a particular branch of production suggests a generalization of the capitalist form, that condition is not necessary for the logic of the model. We could, for example, retain the rate r for branches of production n to s while excluding it from branches t to z. That would mean that commodities n to s, produced in the periphery, are produced by capitalist enterprises (and in this case we could also introduce here techniques $A^c_{ij}L^c_i$, with the rate of wages W^p), whereas commodities t to z are produced by noncapitalist modes but are subjected to capital through their integration in the market. Here we come upon "formal domination." It is easy to show that, in this case, the amount of surplus labor appropriated by the dominant capital is even larger—that is, the super-exploitation is even greater.

Now we can (and must) go beyond the model, which continues to be economic in character. Now, correctly, we bring in the class struggles.

Going beyond the model means, first, taking into account the historical origins of the system. This implies that we are able to define and analyze the precapitalist modes, to observe and analyze the effects of capital's domination of these modes, and so on. Contributions such as those made by Frank, Arrighi, and myself are meant to serve this fundamental purpose. In no case, though, are they more than beginnings. In this sphere, where very little work has so far been done, there is a need for partial, even daring, theses. The discussion has divided us and will go on dividing us, but the progress we are making is clear, because the anti-imperialist problematic is common to us all.

Going beyond the model means, second, appreciating that there are no economic laws that are independent of the class struggle. That is why I have declared that there can be no economic theory of the world economy. For this reason too, I believe, Marx did not write his chapter on the world economy.

Nevertheless some writers, homesick for economics, try to construct such a theory.

Going beyond the model thus means trying to interrelate the class struggle on the world scale, and to make this interrelation operate on an economic base, explaining how these struggles modify this base, in what direction, and so on. This is what I am trying to do, and this is undoubtedly the essential contribution furnished by the Marxists of the Third World—which is, as a rule, poorly understood and badly received in the West. Without repeating all these analyses here, let me recall that I make distinctions among: (a) the imperialist bourgeoisie, which dominates the system as a whole and concentrates to its own advantage a substantial proportion of the surplus labor generated on the world scale; (b) the proletariat of the central countries, which enjoys increases in real wages more or less parallel to increases in the productivity of labor, and, on the whole, accepts the hegemony of social democracy (these two phenomena are interlinked, resulting from the historically completed structure of capitalism with self-centered accumulation, and are bound up with imperialism); (c) the dependent bourgeoisies of the periphery, whose place is defined by the international division of labor and whose anti-imperialist activity modifies this division; (d) the proletariat of the periphery, subjected to super-exploitation by virtue of the incomplete character of the capitalist structure, its historical subordination (its other-directed type of accumulation), and the disconnection derived from this between the price of its labor-power and the productivity of its labor—and which, consequently, is the spearhead of the revolutionary forces on the world scale; (e) the exploited peasantries of the periphery, sometimes subject to dual, articulated exploitation by precapitalist forms and by capital, sometimes directly exploited by capital alone, through formal subordination—thus always super-exploited, and as a result the proletariat's principal potential ally; (f) the exploiting classes of the noncapitalist modes organized in relation to the foregoing.

This extremely simplified presentation illustrates the fact that the principal contradiction, that which governs all the others and the vicissitudes of which largely determine the objective conditions in which the others operate, is the one that counterposes the peoples of the periphery (the proletariat and the exploited peasantry) to imperialist capital and not, of course, the periphery as a whole to the center as a whole.

In the first place, these struggles determine directly and simultaneously the relative prices at which exchange takes place between center and periphery, and the structure of the international division of labor. They determine the orientation and the pace of accumulation at the center, in the periphery, and on the world scale. They thereby condition the struggles waged at the center.

These struggles take place in a domain defined by contrasts and alliances that change from one place to another. The social-democratic alliance (hegemony of imperialism over the working classes at the center) is a constant all through the history of capitalism, except for possible moments of crisis when it can no longer function. Leadership of the national liberation alliance (of proletariat, peasantry, and at least part of the bourgeoisie) is disputed between the popular classes (in which case the entire bourgeoisie goes over to the enemy) and the bourgeoisie (which then succeeds in making imperialism accept new forms of the international division of labor).

These struggles and alliances thus determine (a) the rate of surplus-value on the world scale and the respective (differing) rates at the center and in the periphery; (b) the surplus labor extracted in the subordinated noncapitalist modes; (c) the price structure of the world commodities through which this surplus-value is redistributed (and, in particular, is distributed between imperialist capital and the capital of the dependent bourgeoisies); (d) real wages, on the plane of their world averages and on that of their averages at the center and in the periphery respectively; (e) the amount of rent drawn by the noncapitalist classes (especially in the periphery); (f) the balance of exchange between center and periphery; and (g) the flow of commodities and capital (and consequently the rates of exchange).

The framework of analysis in terms of historical materialism on the world scale implies that we appreciate the worldwide character of commodities (and therefore of value) and the worldwide mobility of capital. These are only tendencies, of course, but they are essential tendencies, since they signify domination by capital on the scale of the system as a whole.

From working out this articulation of the globalized capitalist economy with the national and international social struggles and political conflicts, I have drawn the conclusion that the "North-South conflict" cannot be separated from the conflict between the tendency to reproduce specifically capitalist social relationships, on one side, versus the requirements for socialist transcendence of those relationships, on the other.

4. Unequal Access to the Natural Resources of the Planet

Classic vulgar economics took an interest in natural resources only insofar as they became the object of private appropriation. Such resources were then treated as "factors of production," as such entitling their owners to an income (a rent) determined by its productivity. Contrariwise, Marx analyzes these rents as categories of distribution, that is to say, as shares drawn from aggregate surplus-value. For him, natural resources create no value even though constituting an important foundation of social wealth.

Now that exploitation of the planet's resources has become quite inordinate, whether of those that can be objects of ownership (as, in general, subsoil resources) or of those that cannot (like the atmosphere), we are forced to revisit the question of how to deal with the "natural" conditions of production. Contemporary vulgar economics, nevertheless, remains fixed on its principles, seeking to "integrate" these new "factors of production" into its habitual line of argument in order to "price" them. For my part I go about it quite differently, and I will say so: by extending fearlessly the line of argument initiated by Marx. For the emergence of these questions, precisely, constitutes the finest evidence of the limits that so-called economic science cannot go beyond, and calls on us to deepen the radical critique of, on one side, capitalist reality and, on the other, of its alienated portrayals formulated by the new (so-called "green") vulgar economics, on the other.

The question of natural resources—those of the planet, of course—by its very nature puts the asymmetric globalized system of really existing capitalism/imperialism to the question. The strategies and practices implemented by the dominant centers are endeavors to retain, for their profit, exclusive access to those resources. By this fact imperialist rent takes on a second dimension, superimposed on that drawn from the globalized hierarchy of prices for labor-power.

In the following pages we will take up the totality of these problems, starting with "Mining Rent" (the historical starting point for dealing with the question of natural resources) in order to open up a broader discussion on unowned resources and to conclude by examining the major North-South conflicts over this decisive issue that puts the future of humanity at stake.

5. THEORY AND PRACTICE OF EXTRACTIVE RENT

Does the Marxist theory of ground rent apply to the sphere of *mining*? Here we have the same situation of need for access to natural conditions of production, and of capital sometimes finding itself up against a barrier constituted by property ownership. However, mining presents some obvious special features.

The first of these is the nonrenewability of the resources to be exploited. This feature imposes a specific cost of production that does not enter into rent, namely, the cost of replacement. Under the capitalist system, the operator, the mining capitalist, usually takes this cost into account. But then this factor is determined by the conditions of capitalism's functioning, which means that it is limited in two ways: (1) by the time prospect of the capitalists' calculation of profit, and (2) by the time prospect of the concession by virtue of which they are allowed access to the resource in question. These two limits are usually not independent of each other. Mining capitalists must therefore be sure to put aside an amount sufficient to enable them to continue their activities, at the same rate of profit, when the mines they are working become exhausted. Thus, the mining capitalists devote part of their apparent gross profit (actually, this part is a cost) to exploration for new reserves, both in the area conceded to them and elsewhere. The relatively brief time prospect of the operation reflects the well-known fact that reserves are proportionate to output, and not vice versa: generally speaking, at any moment in history, reserves seem to be sufficient to satisfy no more than a score of years of exploitation.

The cost of this exhaustion of resources for the community is quite different. I have already stated my view that mastery of social development by society itself implies a considerably longer time prospect than that of capitalist calculation, the rationality of which appears, in this respect, to be relative and short-term. When, for example, society grants a concession by an act of state, the problem presents itself like this: when the resource becomes exhausted, the amount set aside for replacement must be adequate to have enabled an investment to be made that is sufficient *either* for a new mine of the same product to be exploited at the same social cost, *or* to substitute for this natural product an artificial substitute of the same use-value and with the same cost, *or*, finally to replace this resource by another productive activity, in another domain (providing different use-values) but regarded as equivalent (that is, producing the same added value).

Some questions still remain open: (1) the uncertain character of such calculations (over a period of fifty years, for instance), an uncertainty that cannot be eliminated in any society, even a socialist one; (2) the problem of how, this being so, a classless society can technically rationalize its collective choices.

Is it necessary to add that this calculation goes beyond the question (which is insoluble anyway) of "external economies and diseconomies". These factors may be allowed for to some extent under capitalism, by means of legislation imposing compensatory taxes.

Is it necessary also to add that nonrenewability is less peculiar to mineral production than it may seem to be? Cultivable soil is not inexhaustible, either, unless it be properly maintained; and the historical experience of capitalism shows, in this case too, how limited is its rationality (the irreversible wastage of soils under capitalism, especially in the periphery, is a fact of history). But there is more to it than that: resources that appear to be inexhaustible (air and water) need—when a certain degree of intensity of industrialization has been reached—to be maintained in the same way as the soil, as has recently been discovered in connection with what is known as the problem of the environment.

The second specific feature of mineral production is of an historical order. Mineral production appears and develops with the development of capitalism, whereas agricultural production, of course, predated capitalism. Capitalist ground rent grafted itself onto a preexistent category, but extractive rent had practically no connection with any antecedent.

Apart from that fact, however, the sphere of mining presents no special features at this stage.

One observes, therefore, in this domain as in that of agriculture, the phenomenon of differential rents. To be sure, these rents find specific forms of expression in mining. The heavy technology employed in mining emphasizes rents of type II (connected with intensification of investment) rather than those of type I. The obstacle to entry into this sector that is constituted by the amount of capital needed causes the differential rents frequently to be combined with monopoly super-profits (in the vulgar sense of the expression) of the sort known as "technological" (which may or may not be temporary) that ought not to be confused, conceptually at least, with rent.

Absolute extractive rent sometimes makes its appearance over and above these costs, differential rents, and super-profits. It is at this level that, with respect to the conditions in which it is formed, determined, and spent, absolute extractive rent offers analogies with as well as specific differences from, ground rent.

Extractive rent, like ground rent, appears when a particular social class controls access to the resources in question. Whenever the owners of the soil also put to advantage their rights over the subsoil, they imposed an extractive rent on the capitalist operators. An example of this is the rent charged for the oilfields of the United States (meaning the absolute rent paid to the owners of the poorest deposits, not differential rents, which are indeed appropriated by those companies that exploit the richer deposits—for example, the ones in the Middle East). Generally, though, in the domain of mining, the capitalist state, acting in the name of the collective interests of the bourgeoisie, while asserting a right of ownership over the subsoil, was satisfied with allowing the dominant sectors of capital more or less free access to these resources in return for merely symbolic royalties.

The same applied on the plane of the world system. Control by the imperialist states over the colonies, and even over states enjoying formal independence, had for a long time the corollary of free access for the monopolies to the natural resources of the periphery, as is shown by the gratuitous concessions granted by the colonial administrations or wrested by means of gunboat diplomacy, or else obtained by paying a mere symbolic royalty, a "baksheesh" falling into the category of capital's overhead costs, rather than rent.

Extractive rent has emerged in recent times, on the plane of the world system, when the states of the periphery have begun trying to impose a real royalty for access to their resources.

At the conceptual level we must distinguish clearly between the *rentier* state and the capitalist firm exploiting the minerals, whether this be foreign or native, even if, in the latter case, it is a state-owned firm. Since the product in question is exported, the conditions of its exploitation, making possible a profit for the operating capital as well as a rent, are determined by the confrontation, on the world scale, between the state that owns the resources and the monopoly capital that dominates the mining activity.

These monopolies are, of course, no more in the position of farmers in agriculture than the states are in the position of landlords. The analogy has its obvious limitations. The superficial formulation of the neoclassicists would speak here of "bilateral monopoly," in contrast to the "pure and perfect" double competition of the farmers and landlords. I prefer to avoid this sort of formal analysis and to describe instead the classes engaged.

At this point we need to ask how the level of extractive rent is determined. Here again we cannot be satisfied with a "spectrum theory," which would state that this rent is situated between zero and the level at which it would absorb the whole of the world's surplus-value.

Vulgar economics is obsessed with the false concept of "true prices," whether for ordinary commodities, for labor, for money, for time, or for natural resources. There are no "true prices" to be "revealed" by the genius of the "market." Prices are the combined products of rates of exploitation of labor (rates of surplus-value), of competition among fragmented capitals and the deduction levied in the form of "oligopoly rents," and of the political and social conditions that govern the division of surplus-value among profits, interest, ground rents, and extractive rents.

Extractive rents are thus determined by the compromises resulting from confrontation between the owners of the subsoil, on one side, and the capitalist class as a whole, on the other. And precisely because the deduction represented by extractive rent involves the overall system of reproduction of capital, the intervention of the public powers has always, in this domain, been decisive.

6. ECOLOGY AND UNSUSTAINABLE DEVELOPMENT

1.

Our Ecological Footprint by Marthis Wackernagel and William Rees (1996), investigated a major strand in radical social thinking about construction of the future. The authors not only defined a new concept—that of an ecological *footprint*—they also developed a *metric* for it, whose units are defined in terms of "global hectares," comparing the biological capacity of societies/countries (their ability to produce and reproduce the conditions for life on the planet) with their consumption of resources made available to them by this bio-capacity.

The authors' conclusions are worrying. At the global level, the bio-capacity of our planet is 2.1 global hectares (gha) per capita (i.e., 13.2 billion gha for 6.3 billion inhabitants). In contrast, the global average for consumption of resources was already—in the mid-1990s—2.7 gha. This "average" masks a gigantic imbalance, the average for the triad (Europe, North America, and Japan) having already reached a multiple on the order of four magnitudes of the global average. A good proportion of the bio-capacity of societies in the South is taken up by and to the advantage of these centers.

In other words, the current expansion of capitalism is destroying the planet and humanity.

This expansion's logical conclusion is either the actual genocide of the peoples of the South—as "overpopulation"—or, at the least, their confinement to ever-increasing poverty. An eco-fascist strand of thought is being developed that gives legitimacy to this type of "final solution" to the problem.

2.

The interest of this work goes beyond its conclusions. For it is a question of a calculation (I use the term "calculation" rather than "discourse"), deliberately put in terms of the use-value of the planet's resources, illustrated through their measurement in global hectares (gha), not in dollars.

The proof is therefore given that social use-value can be the subject of perfectly rational calculation. This proof is decisive in its import, since socialism is defined in terms of a society founded on use-value and not on exchange-value. And defenders of capitalism have always held that socialism is an unreal utopia because—according to them—use-value is not measurable, unless it is conflated with exchange-value (defined in terms of "utility" in vulgar economics).

Recognition of use-value (of which the measurement of economic footprints is but one good example) implies that socialism should be "ecological," indeed can only be ecological, as Altvater proclaims ("solar socialism" or "no socialism"). But it also implies that this recognition is impossible in any capitalist system, even a "reformed" one, as we shall see.

3.

In his time, Marx not only suspected the existence of this problem, he had already expressed it through his rigorous distinction between use-value and wealth, conflated in vulgar economics. Marx explicitly said that the accumulation of capital destroys the natural bases on which that accumulation is built: man (the alien-

ated, exploited, dominated, and oppressed worker) and the earth
(symbol of natural riches at the disposal of humanity). And whatever might be the limitations of this way of putting it, trapped
within its own era, Marx's analysis nonetheless remains an illustration of a clear consciousness (beyond intuition) of the problem, which deserves to be recognized.

It is regrettable, therefore, that the ecologists of our time,
including Wackernagel and Rees, have not read Marx. This would
have allowed them to take their own proposals further, to grasp
their revolutionary import, and, of course, to go further than Marx
himself on this topic.

4.

This deficiency in modern ecology facilitates its capture by the
ideology of vulgar economics, which occupies a dominant position in contemporary society. This capture is already under way
and is, indeed, considerably advanced.

Political ecology (such as that proposed by Alain Lipietz) was
located from the beginning within the gamut of the "pro-social-
ist," political left. Subsequently, "green" movements (and then
political parties) located themselves in the center-left, through
their expressed sympathy with social and international justice,
their critique of "waste," and their concern with the fate of workers and "poor" peoples. But, apart from the diversity of these
movements, we should note that none of them has established a
rigorous relationship between the authentic socialist dimension
necessary to the challenge and the no less necessary ecological
dimension. To achieve this relationship, we should not ignore the
wealth/value distinction emphasized by Marx.

The capture of ecology by vulgar ideology operates on two
levels: on the one hand, by reducing measurement of use-value to
an "improved" measure of exchange-value and, on the other, by

integrating the ecological challenge with the ideology of "consensus." Both these maneuvers undermine the clear realization that ecology and capitalism are, by their nature, in opposition.

5.

This capture of ecological measurement by vulgar economics is making huge strides.

Thousands of young researchers in the United States, and their imitators in Europe, have been mobilized in this cause.

The "ecological costs" are, in this way of thinking, assimilated to external economies.

The vulgar method of measuring cost/benefit in terms of exchange-value (itself conflated with market price) is then used to define a "fair price," integrating external economies and diseconomies.

It goes without saying that the work—reduced to mathematical formulas—done in this traditional area of vulgar economics does not say how the "fair price" calculated could become that of the actual current market. It is presumed, therefore, that fiscal and other "incentives" could be sufficient to bring about this convergence. Any proof that such a convergence would really occur is entirely absent.

In fact, as can already be seen, oligopolies have seized hold of ecology to justify the opening up of new fields to their destructive expansion. Francois Houtart provides a conclusive illustration of this in his work on biofuels. Since then, "green capitalism" has been part of the obligatory discourse of those in positions of power, on both the right and the left, in the triad, and the CEOs of oligopolies. The ecology in question, of course, conforms to the vision known as "weak sustainability" (the notion that it is possible for the market to substitute for all natural resources, none of which is indispensable in defining a sustainable path)—

in other words, the complete commodification of the "rights of access to the planet's resources." Joseph Stiglitz, in a report of the UN commission that he chaired, openly embraced this position at the United Nations General Assembly, June 24–26, 2009, proposing "an auction of the world's resources (fishing rights, licenses to pollute, etc.). This is a proposal that quite simply comes down to sustaining the oligopolies in their ambition to mortgage further the future of the peoples of the South.

6.

The capture of ecological discourse by the political culture of the consensus (a necessary expression of the conception of capitalism as the end of history) is equally well advanced.

This capture has an easy ride. For it is responding to the alienation and illusion that feed the dominant culture, that of capitalism. An easy ride because this culture is actual, and holds a dominant place in the minds of the majority of human beings, in the South as well as the North.

In contrast, the expression of the demands of the socialist counterculture is fraught with difficulty—because socialist culture is not there in front of our eyes. It is part of a future to be invented, a project of civilization, open to the creativity of the imagination. Formulae (such as "socialization through democracy and not through the market" and "the transfer of the decisive level for decision-making from the economic and political levels to that of culture") are not enough, despite their power to pave the way for the historical process of transformation. For what is at stake is a long, "secular" process of societal reconstruction, based on principles other than those of capitalism, in both the North and the South—a process that cannot be "rapid." But the construction of the future, however far away, begins today.

7. THE NORTH-SOUTH CONFLICT OVER ACCESS
TO THE PLANET'S RESOURCES

The question of "Mining Rent," or, more generally, of the income that countries can draw from natural resources situated within their territory, is inseparable from the forms in which imperialist capital imposes its domination over the subordinated periphery. The treatment of this question is hence closely linked to analysis of the phases of imperialism, the international class alliances that associate themselves with it, and the international division of labor that these govern. To each phase thus corresponds a certain simultaneous arrangement of production and demand, an adequate structuring of the distribution of income: grade scaling of prices for labor-power, level and rate of profit, quantity and rate of ground rents, and quantity of income derived from natural resources.

As a first approximation, we distinguish three phases in the evolution of capital accumulation within the imperialist system.

In the course of the first phase (the long nineteenth century up to the 1930s and 1960s, depending on which country or region) the international division of labor, of the colonial type, keeps the periphery confined to exportation of mineral and agricultural products. This division of labor, based on the class alliance between imperialism and the traditional local ruling classes, involves a structure of relative prices for commodities traded at the world level that favors accumulation of industrial capital at the center, permitting wage increases paralleling the development of the productive forces.

The price structures corresponding to this equilibrium offer a place to the ground rents remunerating the landed proprietor allies of imperialism, but have no place for mining rents—the capital of the imperialist monopolies reserving for itself free access to the periphery's subsoil resources and confining development of the bourgeoisie in the dominated regions to its comprador sector.

It is often forgotten that the easy growth of the "thirty glorious years" (1945–1975) was linked to a price for energy (in particular for petroleum) that had fallen to nearly nothing.

The second phase of modern asymmetric globalization begins with the victories of the national liberation movements of the Asian and African countries, "the Bandung era" (1955–1980), and the spread of the Nonaligned Movement. This second phase is characterized by import-substitution industrialization, imposing a renewal of international class alliances and substituting the national bourgeoisie for the former ruling classes.

During this phase, the dynamic equilibrium continues to work mainly on the basis of wage growth, accentuated by the mainte-nance of unequal exchange—the periphery continuing to provide primary materials under conditions of wage stagnation for labor, with which it pays thenceforward for importing industrial capital equipment instead of the consumption goods heretofore imported. Ground rents sometimes disappear when the feudal alliance is smashed by means of bourgeois agrarian reforms that establish new classes of *kulaks* and middle peasants. The ensuing relative reduction of farm prices serves the interests of the local bourgeoisie engaged in import substitution industrialization and also of imperialism, to the extent that those agricultural products continue to be exported toward the center.

Nevertheless, whatever the limits of this first moment of "the awakening of the global South," the movement of the peoples and nations of Bandung did not delay posing the question of the income to be gained by the countries concerned from their natu-ral resources. Bandung proclaimed the principle of exercising national sovereignty over those resources and attained, although belatedly, in 1973, the imposition, as is known, of an upward revi-sion of crude oil prices.

This "readjustment" in the conditions of access to natural resources (of which the crude-oil price is a symbol) was not of an "anti-capitalist" nature. The inclusion of rents (petroleum rents, as it happened) in the price of natural-resource products exported by the South would ameliorate the financial capabilities of the peripheral bourgeoisie and would allow it to embark upon a new stage of industrialization based, this time, on exportation of industrial products toward the centers. The delocalization of certain industries, abandoning the North, by reestablishing a reserve army of the unemployed would allow a simultaneous rising of the rate of profit. The expansion would then be initiated by the Southern export industries, on the basis of which new propulsive industries could resume their expansion in the North. This perspective—whose nature is entirely capitalist—of overcoming the contradictions of the world system constituted the program of the peripheral bourgeoisies at that time.

The imperialist triad rejected all propositions for a "new international economic order," even though the readjustment of crude-oil prices had finally to be accepted. Very diverse theses have been put forward on this subject. Some have accentuated the objective economic conditions of energy production: for example, the trend reversal in the relative cost of crude oil which, after a century of decreases, would have, starting in the 1960s, begun a long-term increasing trend. Others emphasize inter-imperialist contradictions and point to the will of the United States to reverse a situation that was turning against them (dollar crisis, etc.), by mobilizing the oil multinationals and the petroleum-producing states against Europe and Japan. Some even go further and view this collusion as a manifestation of the strategy of the multinationals, which would have chosen to ally themselves with the third-world states against the central states. The aim of the multinationals would have been, by delocalizing the industries under their control, to restore their rate of profit.

The "readjustments" in the Northern economies designed to "absorb the oil shock" did in fact inspire strategies that allowed capital to go back on the offensive and to dismantle the previous gains of their working classes (the postwar social-democratic compromise). These strategies succeeded in imposing on those working classes the structural adjustments needed to allow a restart of the stalled accumulation process.

So the "new order" project finally got under way (the de-localizations are its expression). But it was not under the control of the peripheral bourgeoisie and of their states—and to their profit—as had been envisaged in the original project. It was set in motion by, and to the profit of, the oligopoly capital of the imperialist centers. This operation opened the—short—era of so-called neoliberal globalization, which I have termed a second "belle époque."[4] The rapid and expected exhaustion of this phase of globalization has created the conditions for a "second wave of Southern awakening," beginning even before the financial collapse of 2008.

The ruling classes of the Southern states—or at least of those of them termed "emerging"—have regained the initiative and entered into accelerated industrialization and agricultural "modernization." Pursuit of their enterprise requires that these countries experience a surge in access to the planet's resources even while the cost of exploiting the better among those resources, increasingly rare, has become much higher than it had been. Beyond even these cost questions, the battle has now been contested on the field of access itself to these resources. The imperialist triad intends to keep it to itself—which is necessary to continue its "way of life" and is the basis for the social consensus that assures stability to the power of capital—by the brutal means of military control over the planet. By virtue of that fact, this North-South conflict has become the major conflict of our epoch.

The range of natural resources concerned is far wider than was envisaged even a short time ago. It involves crude oil and natural gas, but equally rare minerals, water, and agricultural land—access to which has been put at stake in conflicts over control and usage—and even the atmosphere (and, through it, the climate).

In these conditions it is impossible to settle the question of determination of extractive rent (or, more generally, the cost of access to the resources in question) in general terms. It must be made the object of concrete analyses of concrete situations. For every mineral, specific circumstances are the conditions for the struggle over its rent, and its possible outcomes. Thus, for a comparative example, one might cite iron ore, long produced only in the developed countries for their steel industries. As the needs of the central steel industries are no longer capable of being supplied by the former big producers, the West has secured itself a "mining belt" composed of secure countries (Canada, Brazil, South Africa, and Australia) that can supply ore at competitive prices in quantities sufficient for the foreseeable future. In these conditions the third-world producers (Venezuela, Mauritania, Guinea, India, Malaysia) are "marginalized" and deprived of negotiating leverage (especially if Brazil goes on refusing to support them). But, on the other side, considerable financial resources are needed to set up third-world steel industries. We see here a possible new association: OPEC countries, China, and the mineral-producing countries. Such an association would reinforce the collective autonomy of the Third World and would dissociate the ore/steel grouping of the periphery from that of the center, whose dominating effect at present is imposed alike over the ore-producing and steel-producing countries of the Third World. In an association of this sort, the "mining rent" would have to be negotiated on a state-to-state basis.

What use, in fact, is to be made of the rent by the countries that would be its beneficiaries obviously depends on the nature of the classes in a dominant position. In the most extreme case—one that is still common—this rent can be entirely wasted by the ruling cliques whose maintenance in power it guarantees, without the popular classes or even the country seeing hide nor hair of it (the rent not being invested in economic development). In other cases—the countries of the Persian Gulf—the rent quite simply goes to feed the globalized financial market controlled by the imperialist oligopolies. These ways of using the rent by stipendiary states or by powerless archaic regimes are, for dominant imperialism, quite acceptable. Contrariwise, when the rent is put to use for development, even capitalist development—as is the case in the emerging countries—conflict becomes inevitable.

8. HAS IMPERIALIST RENT
BEEN CALLED INTO QUESTION?

The visible part of imperialist rent—that which arises from the grade scaling of labor-power prices—is already, in and of itself, gigantic and can be measured by anyone willing to take the trouble to do so. This part can be confiscated by the Southern countries only to the extent that they disconnect themselves—if only relatively—by prioritizing in their development their internal market and the needs of their popular classes. Then, and only then, is the anti-imperialist posture articulated with the initiation of an overstepping of capitalist social relationships and enters on the long road to socialism.

The submerged part of the rent—access to the planet's resources—although not "measurable" (because that access lies outside the field of economics), is no less decisive. Here the battle turns on affirmation of the Southern countries' sovereignty over these resources, together with the commitment to prioritize internal development. Through this choice the Southern countries would reject submission to the perspective of "apartheid on a world scale" whose full extension would be imposed by imperialist logic.

Imperialist rent is quite equally and inseparably linked to the other monopolistic privileges of the imperialist countries, in particular those involving access to technologies (firmly protected by the rules of the World Trade Organization), to communications, and to armaments of massive destruction. Politics here is indissolubly linked to economics, and vice versa.

Through entering on these paths, the Southern nations by their victories would create conditions in the North that would once again challenge the consensus founded on profits deriving from imperialist rent. The advance posts of the Northern peoples are dependent on defeat of the imperialist states in their confrontation with the Southern nations.

Concluding Political Remarks

I will conclude the analysis of the metamorphoses of value that I have projected in this work with a few reflections on their political significance.

1.

Capitalism cannot be reduced to its conceptualization as an "economic system," and still less to that—even more simplistic—of a "market economy." Behind the capital accumulation that governs it looms the active intervention of the market alienation that conditions its deployment. This market alienation is a complex concept, and cannot be reduced to the simplistic formula according to which "markets lay down the law." Alienation takes on multiple forms. It asserts itself across the appearance of capital, and becomes, alongside the other factors of production (labor, nature, science), a "factor of production" on its own. It asserts itself in the illusion that makes the worker who sells his labor-power believe that he is selling his labor. It asserts itself, to a more abstract degree, in the appearance that commodities are produced by commodities without the intervention of labor and that money is itself productive (that money "has babies"), or that time is "productive" ("time is money"). We have met up with each of these facets of capitalism's peculiar alienation at every stage in the analysis of the metamorphoses of value. We have seen that vulgar economics, because it ignores alienation, was by virtue of that fact unable to take full account of the significance of the extension of accumulation. Alienation is the backbone of the ruling class's ideology, becoming (as Gramsci said) the ruling ideology in society, and by that fact an active factor indispensable to the reproduction of the capitalist relations of production.

Equilibrium between supply and demand for the output of each of the two (intensively or extensively) expanding Departments has to be realized from one period to the next, whether that period be taken as short term (one year, for example) or as long-term, the time needed fully to depreciate invested capital equipment (ten years, for example) before its replacement. The expanded equilibrium equations—in values, or after their successive transformations into prices of production, into market prices, and into globalized prices—make it possible to identify the objective conditions necessary for the realization of that equilibrium (the distribution of investments and the labor force between the two Departments and the level of wages, which are functions of the growing productivity of social labor in each of the Departments). Knowledge—possible in such a case—of these conditions might be very useful in a prospective planning of economic reproduction. But capitalism by its nature is ignorant of planification, synonymous with social mastery over the economy. Its economic evolution ("growth") stems from decentralized decisions by the "deciders," the capitalists.

Defenders of the existing order (following Hayek) claim that this decentralized procedure is "efficacious" because it "reveals" the conditions of an equilibrium and, in the last analysis, offers assurance that it will be realized. Contrariwise, Marx proves that capitalism is naturally unstable. Decisions taken at a given moment, themselves occurring in a framework defined by the results of class struggles and interstate conflicts, commit the system to go from disequilibrium to disequilibrium without ever "tending objectively" toward equilibrium.

So bourgeois economic science (conventional vulgar economics), which tasks itself with discovering the conditions under which equilibrium can be realized, is looking for a "right" answer to a false and absurd question. For that reason I have compared it to the question of "the sex of the angels" which theologians of the Middle Ages sought to answer, thus helping themselves better to understand the imaginary world into which they had confined their thoughts. As they fled forward in search of conditions that would offer assurance of stability to a naturally unstable system, conventional economists were forced to invent a concept of "expectations;" the system thus being shaped in its evolution by the "expectations" of its economic actors. It is an immediately obvious and empty observation that enables them to envisage all possible and imaginable developments, and thus to foresee nothing at all. The system tends toward an imaginary equilibrium if expectations are of the sort that would lead it to do so. It would be hard to formulate a finer empty tautology.

Capitalism takes on its completed form only with the realization of its double revolution. On one side is the political revolution affirming the decisive political power of the bourgeoisie (in the successive forms of the, scarcely glorious, English "Glorious Revolution" of 1688, of the American War of Independence, and above all of the French Revolution, which is the starting point for modern politics). On the other the industrial revolution that initiates, with the spread of large-scale industry, its affirmed domination over economic life and the capitalist market alienation through which that domination is expressed. With fully formed capitalism the economic system becomes, for the first time in history, a generalized market system embracing

the products of social labor, labor-power, and the right to ownership of shares in capital. The expression "market economy" con-
ceals the reality of this system, which ought to be called an "economic system of capitalist markets." This form, through which is
expressed the reality of capitalist production relations, is historically novel.

2.

Capitalism is not at all what exists in the imagination of its high
priests. It is only a brief historical parenthesis but yet a decisive
parenthesis. Capitalism went through a long incubation—seven
to ten centuries prior to the French and industrial revolutions—
involving all the Afro-Eurasian societies, from China to the
Middle East to the cities of Italy, until it finally coagulated into its
historic form as European capitalism. The flowering of the capitalist world, its "Schumpeterian" inventive and creative moment,
was short, less than a century from the French and industrial revolutions to the Paris Commune of 1871.

Capitalism then enters on its first long crisis, from 1873 (so
say the economists—I would say from 1871, the date of the
Commune) to 1945. A very long crisis indeed, that Lenin, opti-
mistically, thought would be the last. A crisis whose second
part—from 1914 to 1945—saw successively the First World War,
the Russian Revolution, the 1929 crisis, the rise of Nazism and
imperial Japan, the Second World War, the Chinese revolution,
and the Vietnamese revolution which initiated the liberation of
Asia and Africa. These "events," which can hardly be qualified
as "minor," constituted the "response to that first crisis."

The second long crisis, which started with the U.S. termina-
tion of the international convertibility of the dollar to gold in
1971, has followed a path like that of the first part of the previous
crises: concentration of capitals, forced and violent globalization,

and financialization. It is now entering into its second part, whose
outcome will be shaped by ever-intensifying interstate
conflicts (in particular North versus South) and social struggles. I
refer here to my own work, which suggests viewing these two
crises as parallels.[1] Beyond analogies, it accentuated the qualitative transformations of the system from one crisis to the other, in
particular the emergence of the collective imperialism of the triad
(the United States, Europe, and Japan).

My reading of the history of capitalism meshes with the conclusions that Baran, Sweezy, Magdoff (and, following them, the
Monthly Review team) have drawn from their precocious analysis
of monopoly capitalism. Those conclusions are:

1. Capitalism is, by nature, a system that tends to produce a
    surplus that cannot be invested in the broadening and
    deepening of the productive system.

2.. Economic growth is therefore an exception whose (always
    peculiar) causes have to be discovered in each instance—
    not the rule and effect of the "fundamental rationality"
    of this system, which would by the same token be "without
    alternative" and synonymous with "the end of history."

3. The history of the nineteenth century is that of the instal-
    lation of finished capitalism, spreading in a framework in
    which competitive practices still prevail over monopolistic
    ones: and that those conditions are at the origin of the suc-
    cess of rapid growth in the central economies' system, up
    to the moment when, with the full extension of its
    own capital-centralizing logic, the monopolies abolish the
    former system of competitive capitalism.

4. Since the end of the nineteenth century, with the first
    monopoly capitalism, the tendency to stagnate displays its

tenacious effects, which are overcome only through the parasitic growth of the surplus-absorbing "Department III."

5. Although the first long crisis did not conclude with the disappearance of capitalism, it nonetheless remains true that
the prodigious growth of the "thirty glorious years"
(1945–1975) was brief and finds its explanation in special
conditions produced by the Second World War.

6. The tendency to stagnate, which came back to the surface
with the inception in the 1970s of the second long crisis of
monopoly capitalism, is partly overcome by financialization. The latter is not a "deviation" that might be corrected
by appropriate forms of regulation; it is inseparable from
the survival requirements of the system.

I have extended those analyses initiated by Baran, Sweezy, and
Magdoff in the following four domains:

1. The recognition of the two successive moments of
monopoly capitalism's extension, linked to its two long
crises (1873–1945; 1971 to and beyond the present), and
the identification of the new forms through which are
expressed the deepening of the crisis of the system. This
has become in our day the "late capitalism of generalized,
financialized, and globalized oligopolies."

2. The analysis of the similar ways in which the monopolies
have responded to the challenges posed by each of those
two successive crises: concentration of capitals, financialization, and deepened globalization. Those responses
assured the success of brief, though dazzling, "belle époque"
moments of recovery (successively 1895–1914, then
1991–2008).

3. The passage from the conflict of national imperialisms (permanent until 1945) to the triad's collective imperialism.

4. The recognition of the decisive confrontation, opposing the imperialist triad to the awakening of the Southern nations, which showed itself at the outset through the first wave of revolutions carried out in the name of socialism (from semi-peripheral Russia to the peripheral countries China, Vietnam, and Cuba) and the spread of the Bandung projects (1955–1985). The transformation of the law of value into the law of globalized value gives an account of the nature of the challenge, of the contradictions and limitations in that first wave of attempts to escape from capitalism.

It thus becomes quite plain that an adequate "response to the current crisis" will not be given by the adoption of "effective economic policies" devised by technocrats in the service of capital, nor even by authentically reformist projects proposed by well-meaning leftists.

3.

As I have noted, I did not find satisfying answers in Marx to the question of the globalization of capitalism. I have sought to take up the challenge through recognition of the extraordinary fact that really existing capitalism, in its globalized extension, has produced, reproduced, and unceasingly deepened the centers–peripheries polarization.

I have dared to state that this extraordinary fact governs all struggles and political and social conflicts, at every national scale and at the global scale. I mean by this that both the social struggles of the classes exploited by capital against the exploiting classes (which take many and diverse forms) and the conflicts among the established powers in the centers and the peripheries are intertwined and mutually condition each other. Reduction of this reality, inseparable from the polarization stemming from the global expansion of capitalism, to a simple affirmation of determination "in the last analysis" by the class struggle pitting labor against capital excludes the difficult questions, the true questions, from the field of discussion. Its symmetrical reduction to power struggles, like geopolitical analysis of national policies, is no more worthwhile.

The difficult question involves the struggles of peoples (in the sense of the popular classes), of nations (in the sense of historical realities that have each developed their peculiar personality), and of states (in the sense of powers wielded in the name of these nations by the established ruling classes).

Do they offer the perspective that possibly capitalism can be "caught up" within its bounds and by capitalist methods? Were that possible, no force, no ideology, no cultural project would be capable of seriously hindering its advance. In that case, the "stages of growth" thesis would at last find itself confirmed—certainly not by virtue of the tranquil progression of "globalization" but through the incessantly renewed combat against its forms, from which stems the center–periphery asymmetry. In other words, the anti-imperialist dimension of those struggles would imply no rejection of the capitalist solution but rather the contrary, which is to say the adhesion within capitalism that the nations in question would have sought to impose, and would have succeeded in imposing, on the imperialist powers.

Or these struggles do not open the royal road of a "catch-up" within the system.

Recognition of the globalization of the law of value lets us understand why such a "catch–up" within the system is objectively impossible. From that fact it follows that anti-imperialist struggles are entangled in the struggle for a "different social system" (in the last analysis, for a socialist perspective). This intermeshing is reflected in the competition for "leadership" of the political anti-imperialist fronts between, on the one hand, the established class powers who "naturally" aspire to flourish in the form of national bourgeoisies forcing acceptance of their equal participation in shaping the future of the world and, on the other, the complex and alternative historical blocs centered, to diverse degrees, on the popular classes in the diversity of their expressions.

4.

For the second time in contemporary history the imperialist dimension of capitalism is being challenged. The first time was after the Second World War.

Since 1945, the United States of America, the dominant imperialist power of this epoch, has proclaimed the division of the world into two spheres, that of the "Free World" and that of "Communist Totalitarianism." The reality of the Third World was flagrantly ignored: it was felt to be privileged in belonging to the "free world," as it was "non-communist." "Freedom" was considered as applying only to capital, with complete disregard for the realities of colonial and semi-colonial oppression. The following year Zhdanov, in his famous report (in fact, Stalin's), which led to the setting up of the Cominform (an attenuated form of the Third International), also divided the world into two, the socialist sphere (the USSR and Eastern Europe) and the capitalist one (the rest of the world). The report ignored the contradictions within the capitalist sphere that opposed the imperialist centers to the peoples and nations of the peripheries who were engaged in struggles for their liberation.

The Zhdanov doctrine pursued one main aim: to impose peaceful coexistence and hence to calm the aggressive passions of the United States and its subaltern European and Japanese allies. In exchange, the Soviet Union would accept a low profile, abstaining from interfering in colonial matters that the imperialist powers considered their internal affairs. The liberation movements, including the Chinese revolution, were not supported with any enthusiasm at that time and they carried on by themselves. But their victory (particularly that of China, of course) was to bring about some changes in international power relationships.

Moscow did not perceive this until Bandung, which enabled it, through its support for the countries in conflict with imperialism, to break out of its isolation and become a major actor in world affairs. In a way, it is not wrong to say that the main change in the world system was the result of this first "Awakening of the South." Without this knowledge, the later affirmation of the new "emerging" powers cannot be understood.

The Zhdanov report was accepted without reservation in the European communist parties and in those of Latin America of that era. However, almost immediately it came up against resistance from the communist parties of Asia and the Middle East. This was concealed in the language of that period, for they continued to affirm "the unity of the socialist camp" behind the USSR, but as time went on resistance became more overt with the development of their struggles for regaining independence, particularly after the victory of the Chinese revolution in 1949. To my knowledge no one has ever written a history of the formulation of the alternative theory, which gave full rein to the independent initiatives of the countries of Asia and Africa, later to crystallize at Bandung in 1955 and then in the constitution of the Non-Aligned Movement (from 1960 defined as Asian-African, plus Cuba). The details are buried in the archives of some communist parties (those of China, India, Indonesia, Egypt, Iraq, Iran, and perhaps a few others).

Nevertheless, I can bear personal witness to what happened, having been lucky enough, since 1950, to have participated in one of the groups of reflection that brought together the Egyptian, Iraqi, and Iranian communists and some others. Information about the Chinese debate, inspired by Zhou Enlai, was not made known to us by Comrade Wang (the link with the journal *Révolution*, whose editorial committee included myself) until much later, in 1963. We heard echoes of the Indian debate and the split that it had provoked, which was confirmed afterwards by the constitution of the Communist Party of India (Marxist). We knew that debates within the Indonesian and Filipino communist parties had developed along the same lines.

This history should be written, as it would help people to understand that Bandung did not originate in the heads of the nationalist leaders (Nehru and Sukarno particularly, Nasser rather less) as is implied by contemporary writers. It was the product of a radical leftwing critique that was at that time conducted within the communist parties. The common conclusion of these groups of reflection could be summed up in one sentence: the fight against imperialism brings together, at the world level, the social and political forces whose victories are decisive in opening up possible socialist advances in the contemporary world.

That conclusion, however, left open a crucial question: who was to direct these anti-imperialist battles? To simplify: the bourgeoisie (then called "national"), whom the communists should then support, or a front of popular classes, directed by the communists and not the bourgeoisie (who were anti-national in fact)? The answer to this question often changed and was sometimes confused. In 1945 the communist parties concerned were aligned, based on the conclusion that Stalin had formulated: the bourgeoisie everywhere in the world (in Europe, aligned with the United States, as in the colonial and semi-colonial countries) has "thrown the national flag into the rubbish bin." The communists were therefore the only ones who could assemble a united front of the forces that refused to submit to the imperialist, capitalist, American order.

Mao reached the same conclusion in 1942, but it was only made known to us when his *New Democracy* had been translated into Western languages in 1952. This thesis held that, for the majority of the peoples of the planet, the long road to socialism could only be opened by a "national, popular, democratic, anti-feudal and anti-imperialist revolution run by the communists." The underlying message was that other socialist advances were not on the agenda elsewhere, i.e., in the imperialist centers. They could not possibly take shape until after the peoples of the peripheries had inflicted substantial damage on imperialism.

The triumph of the Chinese revolution confirmed this conclusion. The communist parties of Southeast Asia, in Thailand, Malaysia, and the Philippines in particular, started liberation struggles inspired by the Vietnamese model. Later, in 1964, Che Guevara revealed similar views when he called for "one, two, many Vietnams."

The vanguard proposals for initiatives by the independent and anti-imperialist countries of Asia and Africa, which were formulated by the different communist groups of reflection, were precise and advanced. They are to be found in the Bandung program and that of the Non-Aligned Movement, of which I gave a systematic presentation in my *L'eveil du Sud* (*Awakening of the South*). The proposals focused on the essential need to reconquer control over the accumulation process (through development that is auto-centered and delinked from the world economy).

It so happens that some of these proposals were adopted, although with considerable dilutions in certain countries, from 1955 to 1960, by the governing classes as a whole in both continents. And at the same time the revolutionary struggles waged by all the communist parties of Southeast Asia were defeated (except in Vietnam, of course). The conclusion would seem to be that the "national bourgeoisie" had not exhausted its capacity for anti-imperialist struggle. The Soviet Union also came to that conclusion when it decided to support the non-aligned front, while the imperialist triad declared open warfare against it.

The communists in the countries concerned were then divided between the two tendencies and became involved in painful conflicts that were often confused. Some drew the lesson that it was necessary to "support" the established powers that were battling imperialism, although this support should remain "critical." Moscow gave wind to their sails by inventing the thesis of the "non-capitalist way." Others conserved the essentials of the Maoist thesis, according to which only a front of the popular classes that was independent of the bourgeoisie could lead a successful struggle against imperialism. The conflict between the Chinese communist party and the Soviet Union, which was apparent in 1957 but officially declared in 1960, of course confirmed the second tendency among the Asian and African communists.

However, the potential of the Bandung movement wore out within some fifteen years, emphasizing—if it should be needed—the limits of the anti-imperialist programs of the "national bourgeoisies." Thus the conditions were ripe for the imperialist counter-offensive, the "recompradorization" of the Southern economies, if not—for the most vulnerable—their recolonization.

Nevertheless, as if to give the lie to the thesis of the definitive and absolute impotence of the national bourgeoisies—Bandung having been, according to this vision, just a "passing episode" in the Cold War context—certain countries of the South have been able to impose themselves as "emerging" in the new globalization dominated by imperialism. But "emerging" in what way? Emerging markets open to the expansion of capital of the oligopolies belonging to the imperialist triad? Or emerging nations capable of imposing a genuine revision of the terms of globalization and reducing the power exercised by the oligopolies, while redirecting accumulation to their own national development? The question of the social control of the established powers in the emerging countries (and in other countries of the periphery) and the prospects that this opens up or closes is once again on the agenda. It is a debate that cannot be avoided: what will—or could—be the nature of the "post crisis" world?

The crisis of the late imperialist countries of generalized, financialized, and globalized oligopolies is patent. But even before it passed into the new phase inaugurated by the financial collapse of 2008, people had begun to bestir themselves out of the lethargy that had set in after the first wave of struggles for the emancipation of workers and peoples had worn itself out.

Latin America, which had been absent during the Bandung era (in spite of Cuba's efforts with the Tricontinental), this time seemed even to be in advance of the rest of the movement.

There are of course many important new aspects in the present situation, but the same questions that were being posed in the 1950s are once again on the table. Will the South (emerging countries and others) be capable of taking independent strategic initiatives? Will popular forces be capable of imposing the kind of transformations in the power systems that are necessary for making serious progress? Can bridges be built that associate the anti-imperialist and popular struggles in the South with the progress of a socialist consciousness in the North?

I will refrain from giving quick answers to these difficult questions that only the development of struggles will resolve. But the importance of these discussions, in which the radical intellectuals of our era should commit themselves, must not be underestimated, nor the proposals that might result from such discussions.

The conclusions reached by the groups of reflection of the 1950s formulated the challenge in terms that have remained essentially the same ever since: the peoples of the periphery must undertake national construction (supported by regional plans and those of the South as a whole that are auto-centered and delinked); they cannot take this route unless their struggles are carried out in a socialist perspective; and for this reason they must shed their illusions about the false alternative of "catching up" to the globalized capitalist system. Bandung embodied this independent option but within certain limits, as history revealed.

Could the results be better now, when a second "Awakening of the South" is on the horizon? Above all, will it be possible this time to build convergences between the struggles in the North and in the South? These were lamentably lacking in the Bandung epoch. The peoples of the imperialist centers then aligned behind their imperialist leaders. The social-democratic project of the time would in fact have been difficult to imagine without the imperialist rent that benefited the opulent societies of the North. Bandung and the Non-Aligned Movement were thus seen as just an episode in the Cold War, perhaps even manipulated by Moscow. In the North, there was little understanding of the real dimensions of this first emancipatory wave of the countries of Asia and Africa which, however, was convincing enough for Moscow to give it support.

The challenge of constructing an anti-imperialist internationalism of workers and peoples remains to be tackled.

5.

Socialism (or better, communism) represents a more advanced stage of human civilization, which became conceivable with Marx's initiation of the fundamental critique of capitalism. Given that the invention of the capitalist stage of civilization stumbled for centuries before finding the particular form that assured its triumph, why then reject the idea that the invention of socialism should itself, likewise, be the product of successive waves? In that spirit, I have suggested a reading of the twentieth century— of the revolutions (Russian and Chinese) and of the first instances of Southern awakening (the nations of Africa and Asia)—as a first wave of the affirmation of the objective necessity of socialism, which is the sole alternative to the descent into barbarism implicit in the ongoing extension of historical (and imperialist by its nature) capitalism.

The growing contrast between the dominant center (profiting from imperialist rent) and the dominated peripheries of the historical capitalist system is the origin of the tragedy of the first-wave

revolutions—those of the twentieth century—in the face of conflicting objectives: on one side, to develop the productive forces
whose course had been diverted and whose progress was handi-
capped by imperialist domination and, on the other, to advance in
constructing post capitalist social relationships on the long road
leading to socialism. Once again, the transformation of the world
is being initiated in the periphery of the established system.

Adhesion to the thought of a shoreless Marx does not equip one
with a "crystal ball" that provides infallible foresight. No more does
that adhesion furnish us with a "correct theory" allowing one to put
forth infallible and efficacious strategies (we have seen a fine example
in the twists and turns of the evaluations by communists regarding
the Bandung project). It merely offers analytic tools superior to all
others. Marx has taught us that the paths of history are set by the
results of struggles and conflicts; history is not to be written
before history itself has happened. Marx has likewise taught us that
the solution to the most violent contradictions is to be found either
in going beyond a social system that has become obsolete or else in
the self-destruction of society. Today more than ever the terms of the
alternative are clear: socialism or barbarism. Today more than ever
capitalism's appearance conforms to its reality: a parenthesis in history, the continuance of whose extension can lead only to death.

There are good reasons to think that the nations of Asia,
Africa, and Latin America (a minority comprising 80 percent of
the human race!) will carry it off and will arrive, across what I call
the "second wave of Southern awakening," at putting an end to
imperialist rent. There are likewise good reasons to think that the
Northern peoples—who are not "by nature" wicked devils—
once deprived of the advantages of that rent which until now
made them accept the terms of a "consenting" pro-imperialist
allegiance, will be capable of forming themselves into alternative
historic blocs open to the socialist perspective. The monopoly of
power by the plutocracy that governs them, albeit reinforced, is
not necessarily stable.

Undoubtedly, skeptics will tell us that we are far from having entered on those paths. The constitution of anti-plutocratic/anti-imperialist fronts is not to be seen taking form in the North. No more does one see political forces expressing the interests of the popular classes becoming capable, today, of "overturning" the established powers in the South. Overall, movements of protest and of struggle are still, in the North as in the South, fragmented and defensive. Accordingly, the initiative is still broadly in the sole hands of the established powers, which alone hold the forestage in the North as in the South. But optimism of the will, as Gramsci said, is based on the possibility of going beyond these preliminary stages of the confrontation—indeed, to going forward on the long transition to socialism, "There Is No Alternative."

It will force the peoples of the periphery to learn how to correctly link market and plan. In having recourse—quite inescapably—to the requirements of managing economic development by means of the market, they must keep in mind that in our epoch the "market" is still a "capitalist market" that promotes capitalist social relations and their accompanying alienations. Planification is the only way to lessen the danger of going fatally astray. This planification must not be envisaged as the bureaucratic management of a "state socialism" (in reality a state capitalism "without capitalists," pending its becoming capitalism with capitalists). This planification rest on forms still to be invented and on the active participation by the popular classes in all processes of decision making and methods of management, from the enterprise and from the village up to the nation. In this perspective, market and plan together combine methods at once complementary and conflicting.

This combination will be just as requisite in the developed capitalist societies, whose transformation likewise is not to be conceived as "rapid." Although the methods applied there to this combination will necessarily be different, since the issue is reconversion rather than development, the fundamental principles guiding the invention of the progression of socialization by means of democracy are identical.

Capitalism, far from settling in as the "end of history," constitutes but a brief parenthesis in history. It has realized, in a historically short span, a development of the productive forces broadly sufficient to make realistic as well as conceivable the socialist project of a higher stage of civilization. There is no "escape from the crisis" of capitalism; escape from capitalism, however, is visibly and objectively possible and necessary.

Initiation of the exit from capitalism and entering on the long road to socialism requires, at the outset, the elimination of private property by means of nationalizing the oligopolies—starting with this, the progressive invention of adequate ways to socialize their management becomes conceivable. Reforms not rising to the level of these requirements will remain unable to reduce the destructive power of capitalist management of the oligopolies.

As long as the peoples and nations of the peripheries remain unable to eliminate imperialist rent, or to substantially reduce it, there is small chance that public opinion in the opulent Northern societies will arrive at conceiving the inescapable necessity of nationalizing the oligopolies. Without any pertinence is the argument that the productive forces are still not sufficiently developed to allow for the abolition of capitalist social relationships. The Paris Commune (1871) already disproved that. The "technical" means needed to resolve the material problems of the whole human race already exist. But the logic of capitalism forbids setting them to their needed work. And the conditions of a "global consensus" that would allow this are not in place, as is proven by the recent Copenhagen Conference on climate change. Thus the fact remains that unequal capitalist development on the world scale (that is to say, pauperization of the peripheries) renders inescapable a development of the productive forces oriented in a direction, not of an imitative catch-up, but in a direction allowing for correction of the distortions stemming from imperialist domination of the global system.

Afterword

In the introduction to this work, I recalled that my reading of *Das Kapital* had aroused my enthusiasm yet had given me no greater understanding about the origin of Asian and African "underdevelopment." And I noted that all my subsequent analytical work—during a half-century—has gone into an effort to fill that lacuna.

In my view, Marx's opus remained unfinished. I am certainly not alone in recognizing this. Marx himself, in a letter to Lassalle, wrote: "the whole is divided into six books: 1) Capital, 2) Landed Property, 3) Wage Labor, 4) The State, 5) International Trade, 6) The World Market."[1]

As is well known, Marx published only the first volume of *Das Kapital* in his lifetime. Engels published the (nearly completed) manuscripts of Volumes II and III (parts of which deal with landed property and wage labor) posthumously; and Kautsky later published Marx's notes for Volume IV, which covers the history of theories of surplus value. The contemplated volumes dealing with the state and the system of globalized capitalism were never written.

I am interpreting the "silences" of that unfinished work, *Das Kapital*. I am indebted to Michael Lebowitz, author of *Following*

Marx, for this expression.[2] *Das Kapital*—and here Lebowitz and perhaps several others, like the Englishman E. P. Thompson, share my view—dissects (or "deconstructs") the logic of capital and adduces a critique of political economy (the subtitle of *Das Kapital*). The term "critique" must be understood not as the substitution of a "good" for a "bad" (or, at best, imperfect) economics but as specifying the status of political economy (in the loftiest sense of the term) as the foundation of bourgeois ideology.

This dissection allows Marx to make visible what is concealed in political economy: value and surplus-value, which show up in political economy only in the forms of price and profit. This operation is basic. Without it capitalism cannot be grasped in its reality and so would appear as a "rational" system of organizing production.

Marx thus envisaged completing this side of the analysis of capital with a book on wage-labor (the third book mentioned in the letter to Lassalle). Here Marx envisaged introducing the new class struggle (that of the wage-earning proletariat against the capitalist bourgeoisie) into the construction not of a "political economy" but of a "historical materialism" or "materialist history" (and I do mean materialist, plainly not "economic-determinist"). After all, wage labor is not a "fact of nature," and human beings try to escape from it whenever possible. As Marx points out in discussing the "new colonization" (the settler colonization of North America): the "natural" reproduction of the wage-labor force clashes with the handicap formed by its flight and establishment as independent farmers on conquered territory. Emancipation of those who, under capitalism, are wage laborers subordinate to capital (and exploited by it) comes through the abolition of wage labor (communism), not through its "humane management." The fragments of an analysis of wage labor published in the volumes of *Das Kapital* (supplemented with writings by Marx and Engels from newspaper articles and from their correspondence) clearly point to that intention. But they are no more than an indication; this "silence" would thus probably have been corrected in the third book that never appeared.

Pretty much the same can be said about the second book on "landed property." Capitalism was not produced by "reason's theoretical invention," as the Enlightenment thinkers imagined. Capitalism was built—gradually, then imposed as dominant—through the social struggles of the emerging bourgeoisie against the Old Regime, in concrete historical conditions of time and place, themselves differing from country to country. I have always maintained that the same sort of contradictions were at work elsewhere, from China to the Islamic Middle East. I refer here to my contribution to discussions on "global history" and "globalizations," to my book *Class and Nation*, and to my early criticism of Eurocentrism. But that discussion is only indirectly at issue here. Landed property, as discussed by Marx, is characterized by the transformation of feudal property (with superimposed rights of lords and—serf or free—peasant tenants) into purely capitalist agricultural property. Marx concentrates on that transformation, which he analyzes in some detail in his published writings (*Das Kapital* and other writings). What Marx inferred from this, in regard to ground rent, is discussed by me in this work and is further developed, even "corrected."

But it is only in the *Formen* (*Forms*) that Marx takes up the same question for other—"Asiatic"—societies. This work on precapitalist forms of production—one of Marx's 1857–1858 manuscripts—was only published belatedly (as a complement to the manuscript on principles for a critique of political economy) by Maximilien Rubel.[3] I have rejected those propositions, which indeed Marx neither published nor expanded later. The second book, if it had been written, would perhaps have thrown more light on the subject, but nobody can really know.

Although the fourth book, concerning the state, was also never written, the thought of Marx on this subject can be better understood than on the others. The bourgeois state is a concentrated expression of its economic reality, as Lenin expressed it. By that I mean not that it is solely "capital's state" ("in the service of capital") but that it is also the manager of the "whole," able if necessary to go against a multiplicity of capitalist interests in dealing with the wage-labor force. Still, it's likely that if Marx had written that fourth book he would have told us more on the subject, going beyond his concrete analyses of concrete situations—in particular those involving the nineteenth century political history of France from the 1848 revolution to the Commune. I have put forth several propositions involving a possible theory of the (class) state in societies before capitalism (those which I have termed "tributary"), accentuating the reversal of the relationship between politics and economics accompanying the substitution of the bourgeois state for the tributary state.[4]

My work mainly has bearing on the fifth and sixth of the books promised in his letter to Lassalle. These two books appear to split a single question into two parts: first in terms of "international trade"—the fifth book—and then in terms of the "world market"—the sixth book. At first sight, this is a strange way of going about it. Nevertheless, I have followed in Marx's footsteps on this question. I first (1973) offered a contribution to the discussions about "unequal exchange" in which I specified that this sort of exchange is a relationship between "countries" in which the range of prices for labor-power (real wages) shows a much wider range than that of the productivities of social labor (in the Marxian sense, which is quite different from what bourgeois economists call the "factor-productivity of labor"). Unequal exchange ("North-South," to put it simply) makes up only the visible part of the iceberg. The concept of "imperialist rent," central to the construction of what I call the law of globalized value, implies a deconstruction of everything constituting "globalized capitalist economics." Marx would perhaps have been led to advance some propositions on this subject if he had written that sixth book on "the world market." But obviously we will never know.

So then, could the present work be termed the "sixth book of *Capital*"? If by that we were to understand an "imaginative" exercise bearing on what Marx might have been able to write on the subject, the answer would be no. I have not undertaken in this work an exegesis of Marx's scattered passages dealing with "the world market" (the globalized capitalist system) in order to construct a sixth book as close as possible to what Marx might have written. I have no idea whether he would have discovered the dynamic of polarization or if, on the contrary, he would have emphasized a homogenizing tendency of the globalization process. I put forward, taking off from my analyses of the development of capitalist globalization, an abstract formalization of the globalized law of value which extends that of the law of value. Thus, in other terms, I am, in writing this sort of "sixth book" of *Capital*, deliberately placing myself in the contemporary world, not in that of 1875.

It is for the reader to judge whether this Marxist theory of the world capitalist system and of the law of globalized value is roadworthy, correctly extends the works of Marx, and respects their spirit. In any case, I hope that this publication will give rise to a discussion on the matter.

Notes

CHAPTER ONE: THE FUNDAMENTAL STATUS OF THE LAW OF VALUE

1. On the discussion over "markets" see V. I. Lenin, *Economic Romanticism. On the Market Question*; Rosa Luxemburg, *The Accumulation of Capital* (London: Routledge, 2003)(complete bibliography of the discussion as of that time); Mikhail Tugan-Baranovsky, *The Industrial Crises in England* (first German edition, 1901). My contribution to this discussion is expressed in *Unequal Development* (New York: Monthly Review Press, 1976), 146 ff.

2. E. H. Chamberlin, *The Theory of Monopolistic Competition* (Cambridge, MA: Harvard University Press, 1933); E. H. Chamberlin, *The Theory of Monopolistic Competition*, Boston, 1931; Joan Robinson, *The Economics of Imperfect Competition* (London: Macmillan, 1933); *Imperfect Competition* (London, 1935); Paul Baran and Paul Sweezy, *Monopoly Capital: An Essay on the American Economic and Social Order* (New York: Monthly Review Press, 1966). Baran and Sweezy, *Monopoly Capital*, 1936.

3. Samir Amin, *Obsolescent Capitalism* (London, Zed Books, 2003) 63 ff.

4. *Unequal Development*, 74–76.

5. Ibid., to be found by the reader in *Unequal Development* (pp. 66–98).

6. Samir Amin, *Rereading the Post-War Period* (New York, Monthly Review Press, 1994), 187; *La crise*, 10–12.

7. Samir Amin, *Les défis de la mondialization* ["Challenges of globalization"], ch. IV; *L'avenir de la polarization mondiale* ["The future of global polarization"]. *Capitalism in the Age of Globalization* (London, Zed Books, 1996).

8. *From Capitalism to Civilization* (New Delhi, Tulika Books, 2010).

9. My interventions in these discussions, like the propositions that I have put forward in response to the challenges, are summarized in *From Capitalism to Civilization*, 84–95.

10. On the reduction of progress to GDP growth see my *From Capitalism*

to Civilization, ch. 3, 98 ff.; on the likening of progress to emancipation see my *Eurocentrism* (New York, Monthly Review Press, 2009), introductory chapter.

11. *From Capitalism to Civilization*, 77–84.
12. Samir Amin, *Spectres of Capitalism* (New York, Monthly Review Press, 1998), ch. V, 66–80.

CHAPTER TWO: INTEREST, MONEY, AND THE STATE

1. *Unequal Development*, 66–98.
2. *Unequal Development*, 104–32.
3. *Unequal Development*, 88–112.
4. On this plane, the analyses of S. de Brunhoff, though they stay too close to mere exegesis of Marx where the supply of money is concerned, have very properly reminded us of the close relation between the state and money that is intrinsic to the analysis given in *Capital.*

CHAPTER THREE: GROUND RENT

1. Henri Regnault, *La contradiction foncière* ["The agrarian contradiction"], thesis, Paris, 1975.
2. Samir Amin, *Imperialism and Unequal Development* (New York: Monthly Review Press, 1977), ch. 2.
3. See the history of this development as given by Claude Faure, *Agriculture et mode de production capitaliste* (Paris: Anthropos, 1978).
4. Samir Amin and Kostas Vergopoulos, *La question paysanne et le capitalisme* ["The peasant question and capitalism"] (Paris: Anthropos, 1974); *Imperialisme et développement inégal* (1976); *Le capitalisme et la rente foncière* ["Capitalism and ground rent"], 45–82; Samir Amin et al., *Les luttes paysannes et ouvrières face aux défis du XXIième siècle* ["Peasant and worker struggles confronting the challenges of the 21st century"] (Les Indes Savants, 2005).

CHAPTER FOUR: ACCUMULATION ON A GLOBAL SCALE

1. Samir Amin, *Delinking: Toward a Polycentric World* (London, Zed Books, 1986), 233–297.
2. *Unequal Development*, 104–32.
3. *Unequal Development*, 60-65 and 164–169.
4. *From Capitalism to Civilization*, 11ff.

CONCLUDING POLITICAL REMARKS

1. Samir Amin, *Ending the Crisis of Capitalism or Ending Capitalism in Crisis*, (London, Fahamu Books, 2010).

AFTERWORD

1. Marx to Ferdinand Lassalle, February 22, 1858, http://www.marxistsfr
    .org/archive/marx/works/1858/letters/58_02_22.htm.

2. Michael Lebowitz, *Following Marx: Method, Critique and Crisis* (Leiden:
    Brill, 2009).

3. Marx's Formen is available in English in Eric Hobsbawm, ed., *Pre-
    Capitalist Economic Formations* (London: Lawrence & Wishart, 1965).

4. Samir Amin, *Unequal Development: An Essay on the Social Formations of
    Peripheral Capitalism* (New York: Monthly Review Press, 1976);
    Eurocentrism, second edition (New York: Monthly Review Press, 2009).

PART TWO

Further Comments on Marx's *Capital*
and Historical Capitalism

CHAPTER FIVE

An Explanation of the Algebraic Model Offered in *The Law of Worldwide Value*

Some readers had difficulty understanding what I meant by the letters *e* and *c* used in the model. I offer here some explanations that I hope will help.

1.

In order to understand my presentation, go to the algebraic model:

$$1e + bh = qc \text{ (equation for the production of q units of consumption good "c")}$$

Imagine now a factory producing in a year 1,000,000 meters of cotton fabrics. It employs to that effect 500 workers, 8 hours a day, 250 days a year. The quantity of direct social abstract labor needed is therefore 1,000,000 h, where h stands for one hour of social abstract labor. With respect to what is meant by social abstract labor, and how quantities of concrete labor can be re-measured in quantities of abstract social labor, refer to Part Three of this book, "Essays on Marx's Theory of Value," chapter seven.

Imagine also that the capital (reduced to the equipment "e") needed for the factory has been produced by spending on it 10,000,000 hours of total (direct and indirect) abstract social labor. This equipment operates for a period of 10 years; that is, the capital consumed in a year is estimated at 1,000,000 hours (h) of labor. The equation becomes:

$$1,000,000 \text{ h} + 1,000,000 \text{ h} = 1,000,000 \text{ c (meters of fabrics)}$$

If we assume the hour (h) being paid at one dollar; the production price of the meter of cotton fabrics is 2 dollars.

Now, in order to get an equation that calculates the production price of one unit of that consumption good (that is, one meter of cotton fabric) we should divide each term of the equation by 1,000,000. We have:

$$1e + 1h = 1 \text{ c; or, since } 1e = 1h, \; 1 \text{ h} + 1h = 1 \text{ m}$$

If h = one dollar, one meter m = 2 dollars

Indeed, "e" is a composite of different tools and machines, quite small in size since it indicates the quantity of equipment needed to produce one unit of that consumption good, which is one meter of cotton fabric—because of course there is no factory built to produce only one meter of cotton fabric!

2.

The total direct labor provided in the factory is 1,000,000 hours. The wages paid permit buying consumer goods whose value corresponds to 500,000 hours for their production; the profit (in that value system) also corresponds to 500,000 hours. The rate of profit coming out of this value system is: 500,000/10,000,000, that is, 5 percent.

3.

Phase 2: Technological progress permits the production of two units of that same consumption good (cotton fabrics) with: a) the same quantity of capital (that is, equipment whose annual amortizing value corresponds to 1,000,000 hours); b) less direct labor, say half, that is, 500,000 hours. The equation becomes:

$$1,000,000 \text{ h} + 500,000 \text{ h} = 1,000,000 \text{ meters}$$

Therefore, either the price of the meter of cotton is maintained (2 dollars) and the hour (h) has to increase from 1 to 1.33 dollars, or the wage is maintained (h = 1) and the price of the meter is reduced from 2 to 1.50 dollars.

N.B.

I indicate clearly in Part One of this book that the unit of "e" used in phase 2 is qualitatively different from the unit "e" in the previous phase. Equipment is used to produce not more of the same equipment but a new set of tools and machines that are more efficient. For instance, steam engines are used to produce electric engines.

This appears in the equations for the production of production goods:

$$1e + ah = pe$$

Of course, the equipment (e) produced is different from the equipment used for its production.

This is why I have identified the units of "e" by an index that relates them to the successive phases of accumulation: e_1; e_2 means the value of e in phase 1, in phase 2.

The consumption good "c" can remain unchanged (one meter of the same cotton fabric but produced with a new type of equipment). But it could also have changed and become another quality of cotton fabric. This is why I have used the indices "i" to relate the good "c" to its phase of production: c_1; c_2 means the value of a unit of consumption c in phase 1, 2, etc.

4.

With respect to the length of phases, the shortest phase considered is one year. This is useful since "profits" and taxation are calculated on a yearly basis. Also, a year takes into account the effects of weather on agricultural products, which might result in different quantities of commodities being obtained with the same labor effort. The year basis is useful for considering normal economic conditions. From one year to the next, "e" remains unchanged, as well as "c."

But in order to understand the effects of technological change (the progress of productivity, the development of the productive forces), we have to consider a longer phase, corresponding to the lifetime of the equipment, here 10 years, after which new, more efficient equipment replaces the previous. In this longer time frame, "e" for the second phase is surely different from "e" for the previous one, that is, e_2 is different from e_1.

5.

Section One of this book offers here a kind of a new draft of volume 2 of Capital formulated in an algebraic form.

It is exactly what Marx says in volume 3 of *Capital* with respect to the calculation of production prices. But instead of an approach by successive approximations, I go directly to the equations needed to obtain the system of production prices. The exercise leads to three major conclusions:

1. that the reproduction of the system needs real wages increasing at a rate that can be calculated.
2. that the rate of profit in that case does not tend to fall.
3. that the reproduction in a "pure capitalist system" is possible provided the credit system offers for each successive period a volume of credit that can also be calculated (my answer to Rosa Luxemburg).

6.

Parts One and Two of this book provide together also a kind of new enriched draft of volume 3 of Capital, introducing a third department for the absorption of the "surplus" (as per the Baran/ Sweezy meaning).

Why? Because the normal tendency of capitalism is not to let real wages increase as needed. The means by which this "fatal contradiction" has been overcome cannot be discovered in "theory," but only through a study of history of capitalism. My very simple model (assuming an increase of productivity at the rate of 4.5 percent per annum, and an increase of the wages at the rate of 3.5 percent) produces a result (within 45 years) that is exactly what happened when comparing the distribution of production between the 3 departments for year 1900 and year 2000 for the major set of central countries (United States, United Kingdom, Germany, and France). I am quite happy with this convergence between my model and reality.

THE HYPOTHESES I POSTULATED in order to construct my simple model, as well as the measure of the growth of the relative volume of surplus (in accordance with the Baran/Sweezy concept of surplus) from around 1900 to our time call for some further explanations that I think will be helpful.

I assumed a growth of real wages in the major centers (United States, United Kingdom, Germany, and France) at a rate of 3.5 percent per annum for a time period of 45 years. That growth of real wages was actually achieved during three periods: 1900–1913, 1920–1929, and 1945–1975. The twentieth century, however, included two world wars and the deep crisis of the 1930s. Therefore the reader should understand that it took historical capitalism one full century, and not a half-century, to achieve that increase in real wages (even if menaced today by neo-liberalism).The rate of growth of the productivity of social labor (4.5 percent for 45 years, the results being reached only in the whole century) is not artificially imagined, though establishing proof from current available statistics remains terribly difficult, for the very reasons mentioned in the following paragraphs.

The conventional concept of productivity of the various so-called factors of production (labor, capital, nature, science/technology), conceived as separate from one another, is fallacious and unscientific. In reality productivity is a single integrated unit. In contrast, for Marx there is only one productivity, that of social abstract labor. Labor operates with equipment, on the basis of given natural conditions, and under the conditions of the scientific/technological knowledge available in society at any particular time.

The metrics of the growth of this productivity proceeds from comparing over time the total quantity of social abstract labor (direct and indirect) needed for producing one unchanged unit of use-value. That quantity declines from a first phase of production to the next. There is the additional difficulty of measurement related to the transformation of quantities of concrete labor into abstract labor (see Section Two of this book, chapter seven). Available statistics have not been conceived to facilitate these calculations; these only provide the tools for the management of the economy by capital.

A rough approach to this measure might be obtained by dividing the relevant part of GDP, the part associated with production, that is, the conventional primary and secondary sectors of the economy, plus that part of the tertiary sector directly linked to them (see *Three Essays*, chapter 2, pp. 69–74) by the quantity of labor spent in those sectors. Such a rough calculation would indeed suggest a rate of growth of 4,5 percent for the periods 1900–1913, 1920–1929, 1945–1975 (say, around 45 to 50 years), keeping in mind that these results were in fact spread over a century.

It should be obvious to a Marxist that the rate of growth of productivity of social labor (in accordance with Marx's concept of it) is necessarily higher than that of the growth of real wages. Otherwise, capitalism would not suffer from its fatal contradiction, by which its natural development results in overaccumulation and the need for outlets to absorb the surplus. Liberals would be right: capitalism produces continuous harmonious economic growth!

That being said, the measurement of the surplus is no less difficult than calculating the productivity of social labor, and for the same reason, namely, the irrelevance of available statistics. The sector of GDP usually called "tertiary" amalgamates activities of an absolutely different nature, some directly associated with primary and secondary sectors (transport and marketing of goods

produced in those two sectors), others representing the outlet
for the growing surplus—these activities being for some sectors socially desirable, others not. (Refer to Section Two of this
book, chapter six.) Yet a rough look at the statistics relative to the
components of the tertiary sector indicates that the surplus has
grown from around 10 percent (at a maximum) at the beginning
of the twentieth century to no less than 50 percent today.

That growth corresponds almost exactly to what is derived
from my simple model. I think it gives great relevance to the
exercise.

7.

I repeat as a conclusion of these comments: Parts One and Two
of this book offer a theory of capitalism (just as Marx intended
to do in *Capital*), not an empirical study of historical capitalism.

My theory of capitalism is Marx's theory (in my humble
opinion) enriched (revised) in order to include : (1) a theory
of a worldwide law of value, (2) a theory of the absorption
of the growing surplus in a Department III, which has to be
added to Departments I and II in order to overcome the fatal
contradiction of capitalist accumulation under conditions
of monopoly capitalism. Misunderstanding and uneasy and
unnecessary questions related to the empirical measurement
of indicators result from confusing the theory of capitalism
and the reading of historical capitalisms and reducing them to
one single issue. Those thinkers suffering from a commitment
to the Anglo-Saxon empirical philosophic tradition will always
have difficulty avoiding this confusion since empirical evidence
relates by nature to the deployment of historical capitalism.
The formulation of the theory of capitalism proceeds through
a process of abstraction in accordance with the concepts of
Hegel and Marx.

CHAPTER SIX

The Relevance of Marx's *Capital* Today

I consider Ben Fine and Alfredo Saad-Filho's book *Marx's Capital* (2010) an outstanding contribution, along with the beautiful book of Michael Heinrich, *Comment Lire le Capital* (2015), as well as a few others that present what Marx offered in his major work. I was so much in agreement with these works that I was content simply to praise them and add nothing more.

The fundamental reason for this convergence of views is that the authors understand, again in my humble opinion, that Marx was interested in and focused on the internal contradictions specific to capitalism, thus conceived as a stage in history, not as the end of history.

This handling of the challenge appears in particular in volume 2 of *Capital* where Marx proceeds with an abstract pure capitalist mode of production and identifies the conditions that make possible the working of extended reproduction. By doing so, by identifying those conditions, Marx brings to the forefront the fundamental contradiction of that system, since its internal logic does not permit these conditions being materialized.

Fine and Saad-Filho write: "Marx never draws the implications as in general equilibrium theory that different producers and

152 FURTHER COMMENTS ON MARX'S *CAPITAL*

consumers are harmoniously coordinated through the market at high levels of employment of resources" (p. 57).

Indeed the equations that permit the materialization of the equality of global supply and demand in a dynamic system, characterized by increases in the productivity of social labor, show that this equilibrium implies that the price paid for the labor force (the real wage) increases at a rate that can be calculated, itself being related to the rates of increase of productivity in each of Departments I and II. The algebraic model I offer in Part One of this book (p. 57) indicates how this precise relation can be quantified.

But Marx was certainly not an "economist of the system" keen to prove that capitalism provides a framework that produces a "harmonious" society. Translated into the jargon of conventional economics, "vulgar" economics, Marx writes that generalized markets (of commodities, capital, and labor) produce the harmony associated with a stable long-run equilibrium. Nor was Marx an economic expert advising the ruling class as to what they ought to do to keep the system working, as Keynes did. Marx was a revolutionary, interested exclusively in understanding how the exploited classes could seize this fatal contradiction of the system to push their anti-capitalist strategy.

Marx never subscribed to the nonsense of bourgeois economics, which is part of capital's ideological effort to convince us that generalized markets tend to reveal a stable equilibrium, and therefore that capitalism constitutes the "end of history," with the triumph of a transhistorical rationality. In contrast, Marx shows how the system moves from one stage of disequilibrium to another stage of disequilibrium, in response to class struggles and counterstrategies deployed by the bourgeoisie (including the capitalist orientation of technological innovations) without the system tending to that imagined, and in fact impossible, stable harmony. But as long as we can be convinced to believe in its witchcraft, bourgeois ideology remains the dominant ideology in society.

Indeed, the fundamental contradiction disclosed in volume 2 of *Capital*, that is, the contradiction between the growing social character of production and the private property of the major means of production, and its reflection in the gap that separates the rate of growth of the productivity of the social labor force (higher) from the rate of growth of the price of labor (lower), should be "fatal" and lock capitalism into permanent crisis. Yet this contradiction is continuously overcome, as long as capitalism rules. How? Through different successive and/or associated practices, such as, for instance, the expansion of capitalism through the absorption of pre-capitalist forms of production. These practices cannot be formulated in theory; they are expressions of the deployment of historical capitalism.

Vulgar economics, and in particular its contemporary extreme formulation (neoliberalism), ignores history. It offers a construction of a macroeconomics fully derived from a microeconomics, itself built as the product of the imaginary interaction of free individuals operating in markets in a similar way, all as rational economic maximizers), acting independent of their specific collectivities (capitalists and workers, nationals of different countries, etc.).

The nonsense of this approach, which implies that each of all these individuals are clones, represented by the single Robinson Crusoe who signifies the average economic man and woman, should be obvious for anybody who is respectful of the elementary rules of rationality . As Fine and Saad-Filho write, "Recent mainstream economic theory has given so-called rational expectations a considerable enhanced role in determining the path of the economy" (p. 59). This absurd formulation is at best a tautology—the play of expectations determines the path of development; that is, the short run fluctuations around the stable final harmonious equilibrium But in fact it is closer to witchcraft than to any scientific analysis. The "expectations" are imagined to be those that will produce the desired result!

Those bourgeois economists who did consider the importance of history nonetheless disregarded real history, the history of class struggles and international conflicts, and reduced the historical dimension to mere uncertainty. Keynes, for instance, considers the direction of the development path to be ruled by "waves of optimism or pessimism, rich or poor expectations about business profitability which become self-fulfilling prophecies" (as Fine and Saad-Filho noticed on p. 59). The sense of history developed by Marx and many Marxists after him, such as Rosa Luxemburg, Lenin, and Mao, is far more fertile. And realistic. The reason is simply that bourgeois economists have to convince themselves and others that capitalism is the "end of history," while Marxists are free from that absurd ideological and unrealistic constraint.

Fine and Saad-Filho also offer us outstanding presentations of the major issues treated in *Capital*, such as the composition of capital, the tendency for the rate of profit to fall, the transformation problem, the theory of interest, the agricultural forms of rent. My rigorous reading of Marx on these issues is rigorously similar to theirs, which additionally draws our attention to what is most essential with respect to the method at stake in these areas.

The distinction suggested by the authors between the organic composition of capital, derived from its technical composition, and the value composition is worth pointing out. It helps us to understand that the tendency for the rate of profit to fall is an abstract truth derived from the logic of capital, and not an empirical proposition. Competition, selection of innovations, and practices impacting on the rate of exploitation of labor are means by which capital may continuously overcome, partly or in totality, the fall of the rate of profit. But in their turn, these responses of capital to the challenge create not only uncertainty, but indeed disruption in the pattern of apparent equilibrium (in fact, disequilibrium), and therefore results in a crisis of accumulation. The system moves toward another stage of apparent equilibrium (in fact, a new disequilibrium), and that movement is endless.

With respect to the transformation problem, Fine and Saad-Filho write that "the awkward presentation of Marx can be corrected easily: it is merely a matter of transforming the inputs as well as the outputs simultaneously through a simple algebraic procedure. Commodities have values as well as prices of production and the two distinct accounting systems are possible" (p. 114). This is exactly what I have done in my algebraic model in Part One of this book.

With respect to the theory of interest, Marx rejects the conventional economics in which competition reduces the rate of profit to the rate of interest, thus opening the road for the integration of money, credit, and banking capital as active operators in the process of accumulation. And with respect to the study of absolute agricultural rent, they remind us that, according to Marx, agriculture tends to have a lower organic composition of capital than industry because of the barriers imposed by landed property on the capitalist development in agriculture.

ALL THAT IS UNOBJECTIONABLE as long as the target of Fine and Saad-Filho is merely to offer a panorama of what Marx said in *Capital*, and nothing more. Yet this does not exclude completing the reading of *Capital* and other writings of Marx and eventually correcting shortcomings and expanding the uses of the Marxist method for the understanding of the transformations of capitalism after Marx. That is precisely what I tried to offer to the reader in this book, and also in my essay, "Reading Capital, Reading Historical Capitalisms" (*Monthly Review*, July–August 2016).

Those who rejected Marx's method for the transformation of values into prices noticed (rightly) that the rate of profit in

the accounting system established in prices of production necessarily differs from the rate of profit in the accounting system in
values. They concluded from that observation that the detour in
deriving prices from values is deceiving, unnecessary. Equations
expressing the general equilibrium can be formulated directly
in prices, as Walras and Sraffa did. Fine and Saad-Filho have
not issued an answer to that major anti-Marx argument. I have
done it, explaining that there is no mystery in the fact that the
two rates differ. They must differ, precisely because the process
of exploitation of labor is hidden by the commodity alienation
specific to capitalism, though it is transparent in previous modes
of production. (See Part One of this book, pp. 30–32.)

The developments of Marx on the banking system, credit,
and money as formulated in *Capital* (and other writings) are,
in my opinion, far from offering a consistent Marxist theory
of money. The core of that theory asserts that the demand for
money generates its supply. The banking system offers credit in
response to the demand, itself commanded by the path of accumulation. Hence the supply of money adjusts, or more precisely
can be adjusted, to the need/demand of money. This Marxist
theory of money has been developed after Marx. See in particular the decisive works of Henri Denis (*Histoire de la Pensée
économique*, 1992) and Suzanne de Brunhoff (*La monnaie chez
Marx*, 1967). I have gone a step further, however, and illustrated
how the volume of demand of money needed, associated with
the process of accumulation, can be calculated. The function of
the banking system is precisely to regulate the supply of money
in order that it can be neither smaller nor larger than needed.
To that effect, the banking system operates with a tool box that
includes the regulation of the rate of interest.

Beyond the day-to-day adjustment measures, an efficient
monetary policy should facilitate the stability of the general level
of prices (in spite of the welcome variations of the relative prices
between different commodities, themselves commanded by the

unequal progress of productivities from one industry to another) along with the increase of money wages.

But that management of money does not produces harmony, since it does not impact the central contradiction in capitalism, which is that real wages are not allowed to increase as they should in order to permit the smooth continuation of accumulation. Hence real crises through which that contradiction reveals itself are simultaneously crises in the management of the monetary system. Of course, practices of contemporary management of the financial system in late monopoly capital have more than ever created instruments that function as money, out of the control of the banking system. These innovations in effect annihilate the possibility of an efficient monetary policy. They do not produce any "harmonious" expansion of the financial market but, on the contrary, generate more chaos. I shall not go here into discussing these side questions.

The following observations are also extraneous side questions that I mention here after in order to remind their importance for the reader.

Consider two observations: First, Marx's reflections on money took place in the time of the gold standard, which, by itself, produced a relative stability of the general level of prices. I related the long waves of rising and falling levels of prices not to the famous Kondratieff cycles but more directly to the brutal increase of productivity in the production of gold associated with the discoveries of new mines in the Americas and South Africa. Second, the theory of the active role of money in accumulation that I formulated does not deal with the possible inflation resulting from deficits of public accounts financed by the lending of the Central Bank, which, once the gold standard was abandoned, became easy to implement.

The developments in the theory of the absolute agricultural rent offered in *Capital* constitute only half the picture. Marx also offers a historical approach to the question and looks carefully into some different paths of the capitalist development of agriculture, in particular the French way, which came out of the popular/peasant dimension of the French Revolution, and in contrast, the English way, characterized by the evolution of the old aristocracy maintaining its positions as large modern/capitalist landowners. (See my "Reading Capital, Reading Historical Capitalism"). Hence there is no theory of the absolute agricultural rent that could be formulated in universal terms. The different components of the ruling capitalist social bloc, specific to each of the different capitalist social formations, determine the different patterns of the absolute agricultural rent.

Thus I have reservations with respect to the formulation by Marx relative to the organic composition of capital in agriculture being lower than it is in industry. This assertion was precisely Marx's argument in favor of a general theory of absolute rent. Indeed, landed property may have been an obstacle to early development of capitalism in agriculture. This is no more the case; a full-fledged capitalist agriculture exists now, albeit in different forms such as modern capitalist family farming or large corporate farms. (See my *Ending the Crisis of Capitalism or Ending Capitalism in Crisis*, chapter 5.) As a result of these developments, the organic composition of capital in modern agriculture might be no lower on average then it is for manufacturing industries.

MARX HAD THROWN FULL LIGHT on the central contradiction of capitalism, the one that Paul Sweezy rightly described as fatal, since it cannot find its solution within the fundamental logics of the system. For that reason I wrote that capitalism is a "bracket in history"; it has only created the conditions for it to be removed by communism, conceived as a higher stage of human civilization through a long socialist transition. (See my *Ending the Crisis of Capitalism, or Ending Capitalism in Crisis*, pp. 1-3). Hence Marx remains relevant today, now more than ever.

Therefore, the question that calls for a response is this: How is it that full-fledged industrial capitalism expanded victoriously throughout the nineteenth century, survived its first systemic crisis of senility during the twentieth century, and until this day faces, apparently victoriously, its second long crisis of senility?

The answer cannot be found in the abstract theory of capitalism, but on the ground of the concrete history of its deployment. These two sides of the analysis should not be confused and reduced to one.

After Marx himself, Rosa Luxemburg was the first Marxist thinker who made a serious attempt to answer the question. Paul Zarembka has written two major papers, "Accumulation of Capital: A Century After Lenin and Luxemburg" (Elsevier Sciences, 2000), and "Rosa Luxemburg's Accumulation of Capital: Critics Try to Bury the Message" (Elsevier Sciences, 2002).

Zarembka brings back to our attention the argument of Luxemburg, just as Joan Robinson had done. He then looks carefully into the writings of almost all those who rejected Luxemburg's thesis. No surprise, all the references are to Russian and German Marxists of the twentieth century: Lenin, Kautsky, Bukharin, Panekoek, Tugan Baranaowsky, Otto Bauer, Boudin, Dunayeskaya, Froelich, Grossman, Kowalik, Mattick. With the exception of Joan Robinson and the interventions of Althusser and Sweezy, almost nobody in the West had shown any serious interest in Luxemburg on the issue. This recognition of outstanding writings of Russian and German Marxists is worth notice. In contrast, Fine and Saad-Filho in their book refer almost exclusively to British and U.S. academic Marxians, often additionally influenced by Trotsky's fundamentalism. "Marxian" sounds to me like the name of an academic school of thought. Marxism is something more, uniting theory and revolutionary politics.

The arguments developed by the critics of Luxemburg are weak, to say the least. Lenin's "Notes on Rosa Luxemburg" is far from revealing a correct reading of her arguments. And those

of the others are repetitive and do not go beyond Lenin's analysis of accumulation. My reading of those critics had led me
to conclude that their weakness, shared by Rosa herself as well
as Joan Robinson, results from their confusing abstract theory
and the concrete history of capitalism. (See "Reading Capital,
Reading Historical Capitalisms," where I insist on the necessary
distinction.)

I refer here to the numerical example of expanded accumulation in Part One of this book, pp. 21–23 (both the quote and the
example are on these pages):

> Note that there is no difficulty of absorption. For the absorp-
> tion of consumer goods, the wages paid in each phase . . . make
> it possible to purchase the entire output of Department II in
> the same phase. . . . From this general scheme of expanded
> reproduction I have thus deduced a first important conclusion,
> namely that the dynamic equilibrium requires the existence of a
> credit system that places at the capitalists' disposal the income
> that they will realize during the next phase. This demonstration
> established the status of the Marxist theory of money and gives
> precise content to the Marxist (anti-quantity theory) propo-
> sition that the supply of money adjusts itself to the demand
> for money (to social need) by linking this social need to the
> conditions of accumulation. Moreover this precise integration
> of credit into the theory of accumulation is the only answer to
> the market question raised by Luxemburg.

My example is exactly similar to those offered in volume 2 of
Capital. They both assume that the basic condition that would
permit a smooth accumulation is met. But neither Marx nor I
said that this condition (the growth of real wages at a rate related
to the growth of productivity) is, or even could be realized. On
the contrary, the adjustment is relative and unstable, reached
through economic real and monetary crises.

Of course, the scheme is simplified. The phases identified correspond to the average life of equipment, say ten years. The scheme assumes that replacement occurs for all equipment at the same time, though in fact it happens at different times for different industries. But this complication does not affect the reasoning.

Indeed the fundamental and fatal contradiction of capitalism results in continuous over-accumulation and therefore, capitalism consistently faces a problem of adequate outlets for capitalist production. On that ground, Luxemburg was certainly right. How has this contradiction been overcome in history? Here also Luxemburg was correct: capitalism expanded by destroying pre-capitalist modes of production, both within the societies of the dominant centers and the dominated peripheries. Handicrafts were replaced by manufacturing industries, small shops by supermarkets, and so forth. This process of accumulation by dispossession still goes on with the current privatization of former public services. Simultaneously, these responses of capital to the problem of sufficient demand outlets constitute an efficient counterforce to falling rates of profits.

Rosa Luxemburg did not derive from her analysis of accumulation that the socialist revolution is impossible (or even desirable) as long as capitalism has not completed its conquest of the planet and replaced in the peripheries all pre-capitalist forms of life with full-fledged modern capitalist forms of life similar to what they are in the advanced centers. But both the Social Democrats of the Second International and bourgeois liberals did derive that. Today, liberals assert that capitalism is perhaps in crisis in the old Western centers, but not globally, since it is moving ahead fast elsewhere. Accordingly, they see future capitalism as no longer centered in the West, but rather on new emerging regions of Asia and Latin America. I assert that if this were possible, that is, that the peripheries will catch up and become new centers within the boundaries of capitalism and by capitalist methods, that "no force, no ideology, no cultural project, could be capable of seriously hindering its advances" (*The Law of Worldwide Value*, p. 120). But I add that this is precisely impossible; capitalism in the peripheries will remain subordinate, in spite of its fast deployment. However, the social drama associated with that reality generate repeated anti-imperialist struggles, which are potentially anti-capitalists.

Mature capitalism, facing its systemic crisis (of senility) has drastically changed, through the deployment of the two successive waves of development of monopolies in 1890–1970 and 1970 to this day. This change impacted fundamentally the process of accumulation and the formation of the price system.

I rejected Tugan Baranowsky's roundabout scheme in response to the problems of outlets for capitalist production, associating increasing productivities and stagnant wages. (See Part One of this book, pp. 23-26.) And then asserted that it was Baran and Sweezy, introducing the new concept of surplus, who identified the most important response of capital to the challenge.

Contemporary generalized monopoly capital (GMC), resulting from a qualitatively higher level of centralization of control of capital, has drastically modified the logics of accumulation and the price system (the generalized monopoly price system, or GMPS). The average rate of profit (rather low) has become meaningless. Rather, it is the average between high rates of profits for oligopolies and lower rates for many other producers. Many of the latter are subcontractors who are, in effect, forced by the bargaining power of the oligopolists that buy their products to transfer some of their surplus value to them.

The very simple models that I constructed to that effect (see Part Two of this book, chapter six) illustrate numerically those changes. Moreover, the models give a quantified picture of the monopoly/imperialist rent that corresponds exactly to the evolution that has indeed happened between year 1900 and year 2000.

A final but important observation: The prices in the GMPS have nothing to do with the so-called real prices assigned to competition in the markets, in accordance with the liberal unreal discourse. They constitute a system that simply reflects the capture of the economic and political power by the oligarchies who rule the major oligopolies.

PART THREE

Essays on Marx's Value Theory

CHAPTER SEVEN

Social Value and the Price-Income System

I begin with a personal note. I first read Marx when I was twenty
years of age and then reread him every twenty years at moments
that corresponded to major changes in the course of history. I
read him in 1950, when hidden behind the East-West conflict
and the first Southern awakening was taking shape, revealed in
the 1955 Bandung Conference. In 1970, as director of the African Institute for Economic Development and Planning (IDEP)
in Dakar, I formed the project of making Marx a focus for training and discussion that would contribute to radicalization
of the way forward opened by the African and Asian peoples'
reconquests of their independences. In 1990 the problem Marx
could give guidance to was to know what could be salvaged
from the shipwreck of the twentieth century's historic socialism. In 2010, with the implosion of the capitalist system that
had declared itself the "end of history," Marx's work opened
possibilities for new ways forward whose outcomes are yet to be
discovered. My readings at each of those moments were directed
by my concern to respond to the current challenge. And every
time I discovered that Marx was coming to our aid with incomparable power, though obviously on the condition of extending

the radical social critique he had begun, rather than to be content with exegesis of his texts.

Smith and Ricardo had founded the new political economy upon their discovery of the law of labor value. As thinkers of the rising bourgeoisie, nourished by the Enlightenment and its praise of reason, they found it natural to put labor at the center of the challenge whose meaning they proposed to decipher. Without, for all that, refusing recognition to the merit of the entrepreneurs whose charge it was to organize efficacious labor processes and whose profit was their legitimate compensation.

Marx, contrary to what has often been said, did not endorse this "law of value," even in a better formulated form. His was a more ambitious project: he aimed to found a radical critique of society in general, starting from a critique of the capitalism then building. He discovered that the concept of social value lay at the heart of his project. In any case that is what results from my reading of Marx, which gives high importance to anthropology. In this reading, labor is unique to the human species and is central to the construction of society. Labor as such, and the social value that it produces, are thus transhistoric concepts. Nevertheless, in the successive stages of history the forms of organization of labor display themselves in particular modes of dress. Seeking to understand these forms, Marx discovered different instances of social organization and how each is specifically articulated with each stage of history. The specific instance for the capitalist stage is economic, which becomes dominant over all others. The critique of capitalism is thus the critique of that dominance—by definition an "anti-economism"—whose efficacy is revealed through the reign of economic/mercantile alienation. The concept of social value allows us to discover the historicity of capitalism.

Marx's critique of classical bourgeois political economy (Smith and Ricardo) started from the requirement that, of necessity, the center of gravity of the analysis be shifted from phenomenal appearances (the observed system of prices and incomes; the "market" and the waves agitating the surface of the sea) to the depths of production governed by the law of value and the extraction of surplus-value, which is capitalism's distinctive form for the extraction of surplus labor. Without this shift of analysis from the phenomenal to the essential, from appearances to the hidden reality, no radical critique of capitalism is possible.

From whatever angle we examine society, especially and obviously from the economic angle, human labor is central to all thought. There is no society, whether ancient, contemporary, or future, in which it is possible to abstract from this basic reality. It is this that defines the human being, both as an individual and as a social being. But the particular conditions through which labor shows itself define the particular nature of every society. Marx's intelligence is shown not in understanding this—others had seen this before him—but in his rigorous analysis of those conditions, starting from the capitalism then being formed and then going back in time, reading what they had been in the past (it is human anatomy that allows us to understand—to read—simian anatomy). It was not by chance that the eighteenth century's *Encyclopedia* was the great book of labor—the labor of farmers, of artisans, of the constructors of canals, wells, fortresses, and palaces—described with precision in all its domains. The rising bourgeoisie, despite the limitations of its project for a new class society, could not, in the elaboration of its social thought, fail to understand the central place of labor. I say "social thought" rather than "social science" in order to avoid the trap into which empiricist positivism fell by confusing social and natural sciences.

Once more let me reiterate: at all stages of human history and whatever the social power relations conditioning its workings, labor is inseparable from the scientific and technological knowledge proper to the period and from the natural (ecological) circumstances in which it takes place. To treat these inseparable dimensions as separate is to act like the theologians for whom body and soul are separate substances. Labor is always material, in the sense that its real deliberate actions produce real effects, whether or not embodied in objects, this distinction being secondary not primary as those two forms (embodied and not embodied in objects) are complementary to one another, not alternative.

I therefore consider that the movement of bourgeois social thought toward the rejection of labor's central place is the natural accompaniment of the evolution that turned the triumphant bourgeoisie into a new parasitic class. Thenceforward it was the task of this class to find a way to legitimize idleness. To do this they were compelled to believe that proprietorship in and of itself is the source of proprietary incomes. So the bourgeoisie abstracts from the labor that it exploits to put in its place an invented productivity of time or of money: money "gives birth" (which is true for its owner) without any role for labor and production, without which money can have no "offspring." Marx analyzed that mental process as the form of alienation needed for the bourgeoisie to establish its conception of social reality, and for me that analysis has unequalled power.

The title of economist Piero Sraffa's book—*Production of Commodities by Means of Commodities*—is a fine example of such alienation. Lay on the ground all the commodities considered in Sraffa's model—the finished products, raw materials, food for workers' comsumption—and what happens? Obviously nothing without the labor that puts those things together to transform them into each other. The reality is always commodity production with the help of commodities and *labor*.

Contemporary postmodernist rhetorics continue the discourse of that thought, which has to deny reality in order to replace it with the alienated image needed for its representation of the real. For example, to say that contemporary society is one of services and no longer of material production because tourism and out-of-the-home meals are increasing as a share of

GDP while manufacturing industry declines makes little sense. When reality is examined beneath its immediate appearance these services require a considerable production of things: no tourism without automobiles, airplanes, roads, and railways; no outside meals without restaurants, food-stuffs, and the like.

The disappearance of labor from the scope of bourgeois social thought, sufficient to term that thought decadent (an adjective I have no hesitation in using), is accompanied by an equally strange discourse on the disappearance of the proletariat. A discourse pronounced at the very moment when the opposite process is taking place: accelerated generalizing of proletarianization. This acceleration takes the form of a generalization of wage labor in the centers and the growth of such labor at dizzying speed in the peripheries. Of course, the new generalized proletariat, confronting the generalized monopolies, is segmented. Among other things, it is divided on the one hand between its preponderant forms in the centers, which are implicitly linked to the modes of control of the worldwide system and to the international division of labor, and on the other hand, to its particular forms in the dominated formations. In the centers, an increasing proportion of workers, sellers of their labor power and thus proletarians, find a place in the economic sectors that secure worldwide domination for the globalized capital of the generalized monopolies: research and development in the fabrication of new needs, information and the deformation of information, finance, and military industries. In the peripheries, there coexist a rapidly growing manufacturing proletariat, an impoverished and oppressed peasantry, and a dizzying growth of the mass of workers in what is called the "informal sector."

What we need is not empty and false chatter about the disappearance of the proletariat but concrete analyses of the generalized proletariat's segmentation. For it is only such analyses that allow movement toward an answer to the sole real question: Can this generalized proletariat develop a class consciousness in the Lukácsian sense of being prepared for the challenge of becoming the universal class, an actor in the project of a classless society, bearer of a communism understood as a higher stage of civilization? I do say "become," since the observation of reality suggests no such thing. The consciousnesses (not consciousness) of belonging to defined social groups (and not to the generalized proletarian class) hold sway. Is it possible to go beyond this infantile stage of social consciousness? Or is that only a utopian (in the banal sense of impossible) wish because it would be foreign to, if not in conflict with, human nature? Bourgeois social thought tries to make us think so, by substituting for Marx's anthropology the anthropology of geneticism or psychologism by way of arguments that seem very weak to me. Marxism, understood not as exegesis of Marx but as the effort to analyze reality critically in order to transform it, seems to me to be by far the most effective toolkit for advancing in response to the challenge, both by thought (inventive and creative in imagination, accurate in concrete analysis) and by action (identification of strategic objectives for the struggle at each stage of its development). Marxism is not outlived; on the contrary, it is more necessary than ever. That does not make me see in Marxism a religion revealed for all time to come. No, by applying Marxism to Marxism we will understand that it will necessarily be surpassed if and when humanity reaches communism, the higher, classless-society stage of civilization. Meanwhile Marxism remains the most effective social thought, therefore the most scientific, for understand-ing class society and acting to dismantle it.

The divergences thus separating what is produced by the workings of "the market" (a weak term that hides the capitalist relationships framing it) from what the higher logic of social value puts to work do not show Marx's "mistake." On the contrary, they show the whole radical critical bearing of his project, and the success of his demonstration of capital-ism's historical nature.

In this study I will put forward an overall picture of the divergences separating the capitalist system's observed system of prices and incomes from one corresponding to such values as those defined by Marx.

The operative forces determining those gaps did not remain unchanged and self-identical throughout the nineteenth and twentieth centuries, and because of this it is important to specify the particular characteristics of each successive phase the capitalist system went through as it unfolded into its finished form, from the Industrial Revolution, starting from the close of the eighteenth century, to our own time, and to identify the nature of the forces to be con-sidered as their activity manifested.

In other respects, these forces show their particular individual aspects according to whether we are dealing with a particular historical social formation (Victorian England, the German Empire from 1870 to 1914, the United States before or after the Civil War, British India, the Ottoman Empire or the Egypt of the nineteenth century, colonial Africa, the countries of today's European Union, or today's emerging countries) or whether we are dealing with the globalized capitalist system at a particular moment of its history (1840, or 1880, or 1930, or 2010). So what counts is to specify the field of play—local or global—in which those different forces operated.

The way in which social value, as formulated by Marx, operates expresses the rationality of a choice of production of definite use-values based on their measure of social utility, which is to say, their usefulness for human society. This rationality transcends such rationality as rules the reproduction of the capitalist mode of production. Capitalist rationality is that which governs the accumulation of capital, based as it is on the extraction of surplus value. Economic decisions are made not by society, but by the capitalists. The system of prices and incomes frames the operative rationality of those decisions. So economic decisions taken in the framework of the empirical system of prices and incomes (themselves de-fined by the division of the produced value—termed "value added"—between wages and profits) will be different from those that might be made in a framework that respects the demands of the law of social value, which defines, in the coming socialism, the principle of collective social management over economic decisions.

The general social and historical outlook of the bourgeoisie (its *Weltanschauung*) requires belief that capitalism is natural. To that end, bourgeois economic theory attempts to demonstrate that the mode of decision making within the framework of the empirical system of prices and incomes results in a rational allocation of resources (capital and labor) identical to an optimal chosen output of social use values. But it can do so only by way of a succession of tautological arguments involving productivities ascribed to the different "factors of production" (capital and labor), in contrast to Marx's concept of the only existing productivity, that of social labor.

This fundamental difference involving the view of social reality and, consequently, the scientific method needed for its analysis, stems from the contrast between two anthropologies. Marx's conception therefore links the rigorous analysis of the apparent laws governing reproduction of the capitalist mode of production (as given, moreover, at a single moment and place of its spread) to analysis of the totality of forces fashioning social structures and determining their evolution, which make up the object of study for historical materialism.

I will say more about these general conclusions at the end of this essay, which will proceed based on concrete evaluation of the different reasons governing the referred-to system of values/ system of prices and incomes divergences, and on evaluation of the functioning of the forces called on to locate and define those reasons.

To start with, I will put forward, pell-mell, a rapid enumeration of the reasons governing those divergences:

1) landed property and rent;

2) control over money capital and the rate of interest;

3) the mobility of capitals and the transformation of values into prices of production;

4) changes, linked to the transformation of capitalism into monopoly capitalism, of the price-determination system;

5) regulation of the price system operative in a monetary system based on commodity money (metal, especially gold);

6) change from that regulation, linked to abandonment of the gold standard;

7) divergence between measurement of social labor as defined in terms of abstract labor and the empirical wage scale;

8) the transformation of the price system required to move from the analysis of a local (national) social formation to that of the global capitalist system linking the dominant central formations to dominated peripheral formations in an unequal interdependence;

9) the effects on the price system of the "financial excrescence," that is, the appraisal of the "value" of a "capital" through that of the stock certificates representing the private appropriation of that "capital" (the quotation marks will be explained further on in my discussion of this matter).

I have already expressed my views on each of those nine selected topics in various old or recent writings. I will recall those writings throughout the following discussions and in the concluding references. But for that reason it seems useful here to put forward a synthesis of them. Each of the reasons for the divergence separating empirical reality from the fundament of the system expressed by the law of social value—in other words, the modus operandi of the latter—is unique. Some have been working continuously over the course of those two centuries, although in conditions of time and place that shaped the particular ways in which they were expressed. Others appear only with the passage from one stage of capitalist development to the next: especially with the passage from "competitive" (the meaning of the quotation marks will be explained) capitalism to monopoly capitalism, and then from its preliminary form (from 1900 to 1970) to what I call "contemporary capitalism of generalized, financialized, and globalized monopolies" (the meaning of which expression will likewise be explained).

I have adopted a historical presentation of my observations and conclusions, dividing this history among the three successive stages of its unfolding: 1) nineteenth-century competitive capitalism; 2) the primary (1900–1970) stage of monopoly capitalism; 3) contemporary (post-1975) generalized-monopoly capitalism. The advantage of this presentation is to allow articulation of the different mechanisms for those enumerated divergences and to illuminate the holistic nature of their workings: in other words, integrate into a broader historical materialist outlook the economic laws governing each chronologically limited stage of capitalism.

This method can be carried out ad infinitum by looking at slices of time as short as desired and at equally precise localities. To do so would be to write a history of capitalism, and that is not the object of this infinitely more modest work. May the reader excuse what might be considered oversimplifications, which I hope will not be so outrageous as to invalidate its conclusions.

In the course of this short text, I will put special emphasis on the hot subjects that not only have caused critics of Marx to spill much ink but likewise have given rise to stormy debates among Marxists: transformation from value to price, abstract labor, productive and unproductive labor, the law of the tendency of profit, the nature of money, the definition of use value, general economic equilibrium, the question of surplus. The shortness of this work compels me to offer formulations that might well appear brusque, especially to a reader not familiar with the elaborations on these questions that I have made elsewhere and to which I shall make only brief references. In any case, I do not offer them in a polem-ical spirit. I do not insult those who read Marx differently than I do. I wish only for a deepening of our debates; my only concern is to give an impulse to the struggles for emancipation of workers and peoples.

NINETEENTH-CENTURY COMPETITIVE CAPITALISM

The fashionable legend claims that industrial capitalism belongs to an outlived past and that contemporary capitalism henceforward will be based on services and no longer on material production, in place of which would be substituted a capitalism termed cognitive. I will not reiterate here what I have already written about this dubious rhetoric, but not at the price of neglecting the gigantic transformations separating our capitalism from that of the nineteenth century. Perhaps for lack of semantic imagination, I will term nineteenth-century capitalism "concrete" and that of our contemporary world "abstract."

Capitalism, in the completed form it took starting with the Industrial Revolution and in its extension during the nineteenth century, corresponded to a concrete historical reality whose dimensions are crucial to an understanding of its operational logic. The new class, having mastery over economic development and rising steadily to a position of class dominance over the political system, was made up of men and of families linked to determinate and defined economic entities; they were owners of capital (or of its essential elements), of factories, trading houses, specialized financial firms. They made up "concrete bourgeoisies," exercising economic management directly through their private property. This was management through effective competition among capitals (and thus among the capitalists, the bourgeois). This is the concrete competition that Marx analyzes to under-stand the transformation of the system of values into a system of prices.

Mid-nineteenth-century capitalism, in what Marx knew as the norms and conditions of its establishment in developed Europe (England and Scotland, France, Belgium, the Rhineland, New England), is properly termed "concrete" inasmuch as it was embodied in visible social realities: the bourgeois, himself owner of the physical production sites. Property over means of production grouped in the producing enterprises was personal, familial, or involved only a few associated bourgeois. There were multiple and scattered places in which capitalist production relations were crystallized: there were ironmongers, coal-mine owners, textile mills, trading houses, and banks, each having its unique owner.

Competition among capitalists (and thus among the diversely owned capitals) was real and dependent on two orders of logics. There was competition among firms in the same field, competing in production of use values: competition within groups of spinners, weavers, coal mines, trading houses. This competition forced them into innovative techniques of production: the introduction of more efficient machines and more effective ways to organize labor. But it must be recognized that the rationality of this calculation, aiming to reduce the production cost for each unit of use value output, does not produce the same results as those that would stem from a calculation whose objective would be to reduce the social cost of that output as measured by the quantity of abstract social labor expended to that purpose.

But there was likewise competition among branches producing different use values. Surplus value, proportional to the volume of direct labor put to work, was to take form as profit through the division of capitals among branches of production of differing organic composition, that is, of different ratios of constant (non-labor inputs) to variable capital (labor). This was the notorious transformation of values into prices of production.

Marx deals with these two fields of competition among capitals, which enable the passage from values to prices of production and to market prices. That treatment calls for specifications about the nature of Marx's project, the productivity of social labor, the question of the transformation of values into prices of production, the concept of abstract labor, and the trend over time of the rate of profit.

Marx's Project

Marx's project, in his critical analysis of capital, was to separate out the mode of operation of the capitalist law of value masked by the appearance of the workings of markets. That choice is obviously incomprehensible to bourgeois economics, which, in its characteristic spirit of formal logic and empiricist positivism, thinks it can directly grasp "reality."

Marx's project is of another sort, to be grasped only by understanding the meaning of *Capital*'s subtitle, *Critique of Political Economy*. This critique consists not in substituting a "good economic theory" for another one judged bad or inadequate, but in shining light on the status of this new science. Marx is answering a new question, put by him alone: In what kind of society is this new economic science the product? What social vision allowed it to emerge, and what are the limits within which that vision confines it? Marx discovered the specific nature of capitalism, in contrast to the ways in which earlier societies were organized. This nature inheres in the fact that the economic factor is not merely "determining in the last resort" but that it becomes the directly dominant factor. Because of this, economics becomes independent, freeing itself from its previous subordination to the political/ideological factor characteristic of previous regimes. Economic and mercantile alienation, proper to capitalism, now gives a new status—that of an objective reality governed by "laws" working in society like external forces—to the practices governing the reproduction of the economic system. The space is cleared for constitution of a new science, whose aim is to discover those "laws."

Marx's ambition, beyond discovery of those "laws," was wider yet. He aimed to place those apparent laws governing capitalism in a more ample historical panorama, transcending capitalism. To do that, he had to go roundabout, by way of the analysis of social labor and of value. This detour allowed him to understand how under capitalism social labor takes on forms different from those expressed in previous periods, how under capitalism social labor is dominated by capital (exploited) and how the apparent laws governing accumulation (the appreciation of capital) conceal that domination. In other words, how the product of the exploitation of social labor takes the form of profits for different segments of capital and of property owned and controlled by the new, bourgeois dominating class. The transformation of values into prices is at the heart of that analysis.

The Productivity of Social Labor

In Marx's analysis, there exists only one "productivity," which is social labor defined by the quantities of abstract labor contained in the commodity product turned out by a collective of workers.

The productivity of social labor is improved whenever society, to produce a definite unit of use value, can devote to that end a lesser quantity of abstract (direct and indirect) labor. Such improvement is the result of progress in the technologies put into operation on the basis of society's scientific knowledge. The productivities of social labor can be compared in two production units outputting the same use value; it is meaningless to compare productivities of social labor in two branches of production outputting different use values. So comparing the general productivity of social labor in two successive periods of capitalist development (or, more broadly, of historical development), or of two systems (two countries, for example), occurs through analogical reasoning. The measurement of this general productivity is obtained by calculating the weighted average of progress in productivity in the different branches of production of analogous use values. This is an approximate calculation, since the number of use values in the total to be considered is always much higher than the number that can be taken into account and the weighting itself is in part dependent on the evolution of productivities in each of the branches considered.

As I have said, the law of value formulated by Marx, based on the concept of abstract labor, expresses the rationality of the social utility of a definite use value. This rationality is not that which governs the reproduction, ordered by the extraction of surplus value, of the capitalist mode of production. Although the system of values is independent of the rate of extraction of surplus value, the system of prices itself is inseparable from the distribution of incomes, Piero Sraffa failed in his attempt to define a unit of measure that would let him free the price structure from its dependance in regard to distribution.

Bourgeois economic theory, which claims that the market through which prices are expressed produces a rational allocation of resources, arrives at this notion only by artificially carving up productivity into "components" ascribed to each of the "factors of production." Although this partitioning is devoid of scientific value and is based merely on tautological arguments, it is "useful" because it is the only way to legitimize capital's profit. The method utilized by this bourgeois economics to determine the "wage," as the marginal productivity of the "last worker hired," stems from the same tautology and shatters the unity of the collective, the only creator of value. Moreover, contrary to the unproven assertions of conventional economics, employers do not make their decisions by way of this "marginal calculation."

Progress in the productivity of social labor expresses itself through reduction in the quantity of abstract labor needed to produce one unit of the same use value. So it is necessary to identify this unit. Empirically, this is surely not too difficult: meters of cloth, or tons of cement, an automobile of a given horsepower, so many hours of babysitting, a particular type of doctor's examination, etc. To grasp the progress of productivity for their production is generally easy in the short to medium term (up to a few years). This year's model of an automobile has a use value analogous to that of last year. We thus can measure the gain in productivity from one year to another, and going back in time by short stages—in economic calculation this is called measurement "in constant prices"—conclude that productivity has doubled over, say, thirty years. But by going back in time this way, the changes that define the use value at issue are ignored. Take, for example, transportation. By airplane, a human being can be carried a distance of 15,000 km in one day. A hundred and fifty years ago, to cover that distance by coach and sailing ship would have taken a full year, 365 times as long. Can one say that the airplane is 365 times more efficacious (and treat that effectiveness as productivity) than the coach-ship complex of yesteryear? Or should one compare the duration of social labor needed today to produce an airplane (and divide that time by the number of passenger-kilometers transported in one year) to that which was necessary in that time to produce the coach and the ship (divided in like fashion)? This is an exercise that is nearly impossible, and moreover is useless, because the use values at issue are no longer the same, nor the needs underlying them.

Marx pointed out, rightly, that consumption modes are not prior givens in regard to production decisions, but that, contrariwise, it is production that gives its orders to consumption.

In some domains measurement of "productivity gains" is even more problematic, conventional, even illusory and deceptive, because the use values being compared are not comparable. Can one say that today's medicine is "one-and-a-half times" as efficacious or "productive" as that of a century ago if, over that span, longevity has increased by 50 percent? For example, the increasing cost of health is measured, from year to year, as its percentage of the total expenditures making up the GDP. But it is known that the same proportions of the latter (comparable between the United States and Western Europe) give different outcomes. So there are other criteria of social choice that cannot be reduced to the choices set forth by supposed economic (capitalist in this case) rationality.

The Transformation Problem

Much ink has been spilled on account of the transformation problem. Transformation indeed involves a necessary difference between the rate of profit as measured in the system of prices of production and that drawn from the system of values. This discrepancy has been treated by economists as proof of the failure of Marx's conception of transformation. In contradistinction, I have said and repeated that this difference was, to the contrary, expectable and necessary for anyone who does not, miles away from Marx's thought and from his distinction between immediate phenomenal appearances and the essential material reality behind them, reduce scientific analysis to direct empirical observation. If the two rates of profit at issue were identical, the exploitation of labor in the forms characteristic of capitalism would be as transparent as it was in previous epochs. A serf works three days on his land and three on that of his lord; the rate of surplus labor drawn from the serf's exploitation is immediately visible. Under capitalism exploitation is made opaque by the generalized commodity form of social relationships: the proletarian sells his labor power, not his labor. That opacity is given expression by the difference between the two rates.

The analysis, then, of the realization conditions for expanded accumulation that Marx carries out in the second volume of

Capital, is based, quite logically, on the distinction between two departments of production, one the producer of capital goods, the other of consumer goods. This analysis centers its attention on the segment of the productive system directly governed by the capitalist mode. It is not a matter of a theory of general supply/demand equilibrium comparable and analogous to those (Walrasian or Sraffian) of bourgeois economics. For in its evolution, the rate of surplus value is subject to the results of working-class struggles and to the mode of expansion of the capitalist segment of the productive system, which absorbs (or subordinates) the other (peasant and artisan) forms of commodity production. As a whole, the system does not tend toward an equilibrium that can be predefined but rather goes from disequilibrium to disequilibrium. Marx's analysis, unlike that of bourgeois economics, is not economic determinist; its place is in the much wider field of historical materialism.

Marx had built his critique of capitalism, and of the economic theory legitimizing its extension, during the competitive-capitalism epoch of the nineteenth century. The theory of value and that of the transformation of the system of values into a system of prices made up the central axis of that critique. Bourgeois economists before Marx (the vulgar economics of Say, Bastiat et al.) and above all after him put their efforts to an attempted demonstration that subjection of society to the requirements of generalized competitive markets would result in a general equilibrium favoring progress for all, at national and global levels. The two great attempts at such a demonstration (by Walras and by Sraffa) failed to do so (see Part One). Moreover, the reality of the global system has shown that capitalism does not result in homogenization of economic conditions at that level but, on the contrary, produces increasing polarization.

The Concept of Abstract Labor

The concept of abstract labor, formulated by Marx, defines the common denominator allowing the addition of different forms of simple (unskilled) and complex (skilled) labor. The unit of abstract labor is a composite unit linking, in given proportions, units of simple (without skill) and complex (skilled) labor. Simple (unskilled) and complex (requiring training) labor are easy to understand. But the concept of abstract labor is not directly visible. Now, the products of a society are not the work of laborers isolated from each other but of a collective, apart from which neither the least skilled nor the most highly skilled labor has any meaning: their contributions together are what make those products.

Can an hour worked by an engineer and one by a laborer be regarded as contributing equal amounts to the produced value? And if not, in what proportions? Bourgeois economics, ignoring value through confusing it with (what is called market) price, dodges the question: for it, the different wages of the engineer and the laborer reflect the unequal social utility of their contributions. Which is to beg the question with a pure and simple tautology, putting recognition in place of explanation.

I have proposed a way to calculate the proportions ordering the differing contributions to value formation, based on accounting for the training time needed to produce skilled workers and recovery of the cost of such training over the working life of such a skilled worker. This method would justify a wage ratio (skilled wage divided by unskilled wage) of one to one and a half or two, hardly more. This method seems to me to be consonant with that of Marx and would allow reduction of complex (skilled) labor to simple labor. (I refer the reader to Chapter Five of this book for details.)

Now, the empirical wage scale is much broader than that which would be suggested by the operations of the abstract-labor concept. Thus, this concept does not explain the empirical wage scale deriving, in the world such as it is, from the long history of inequality and differently valued social statuses, and from the relative poverty (remaining even in the rich countries) of shareable wealth. The attempt to legitimize this hierarchy as expressing the marginal productivities of the work done by different categories of worker is tautological. Capitalism's ideology always valorizes inequality, whether of wages or as expressed in capital wealth, by arguments that make inequality the source of progress. Reality makes clear that solidarity has a more important role, in achieving not only social progress (trade unions) but also, likewise, the progress of sciences and technologies in all historical ages.

If the wage scale for different categories of skilled workers extends over a broad span, going, let us say, from 1.5 to 2 times subsistence (the unskilled wage) for many, 3 to 4 times for some, and a much higher multiple for a small minority termed "extra-skilled," it will be recognized that though the majority of workers contribute to the formation of surplus value, albeit in differing proportions—and in this sense the expression "super-exploited" in regard to the two-thirds majority of wage earners is quite meaningful—there exists also a category of the supposed "super-skilled" (and they may sometimes really be so) who consume more surplus value than that to which their labor contributes.

An empiricist mind might believe that the unit of abstract labor can be calculated on the basis of the observed wage scale by taking the weighted average of actual wages. For my part, I consider this operation forbidden by the concept of abstract labor. The observed divergence is no proof of Marx committing yet another logical error; on the contrary, the recognition of this divergence allows location of the relativity of the supposed rationality of class society.

Capitalism's characteristic fundamental inequality in the distribution of income rests in the first instance on the contrast opposing the power of the owners of capital to the subordination of the sellers of labor power. The wage scale comes as a supplement. But the latter has acquired a new dimension. The contemporary system of generalized-monopoly capital is based on extreme centralization in the control of capital, accompanied by a generalization of wage labor. In these conditions a large fraction of profit is disguised in the form of wages (or quasi-wages) of the higher levels of the middle classes who are employed as servants of capital. Thus the separations among the formation of value, the extraction of surplus-value, and the distribution of the surplus value become yet wider.

But what of the hierarchy of remunerations in a distant future? In that future will there still have to be engineers and laborers? The materialist dialectic of the coming evolution will give its answer to the question and at present the diverse possibilities can only be glimpsed by imagination alone. Reflection on that question illuminates the fallacious character of ascribing an absolute character to the capitalist system's rationality. The bourgeois economist's absolute rationality becomes relative in the temporal space extending beyond capitalism as a historical phase. On that scale it can even become irrationality, as we will see, for example, in dealing with natural resources.

TRENDING EVOLUTION OF THE RATE OF PROFIT

Marx's schemas of expanded reproduction allow quantitative specification of the rate of growth in wages needed for the realization of accumulation, a rate that is defined by the rates of productivity growth in each of the two departments, I and II. If this condition is fulfilled, the rate of profit is in turn defined and, as I have shown elsewhere, does not necessarily exhibit a downward tendency. That would require an increase in the organic composition of capital expressed in a price of production linked to a rate of surplus value that is not itself increasing notably.

Is Marx's intuition, suggesting that such is the case, well founded? Yes, insofar as increasing productivity involves not production of the same capital goods in increasing quantity (the model of extensive growth without progress in productivity) but innovation, that is, the production of new capital goods. At the same time the extension of capitalist social relations, the relationships through which the power of capital is expressed, reduces the capability of workers to gain the level of wage increases required to assure the dynamic equilibrium of accumulation. Thus the major countertendency to the fall in the rate of profit is at work in a real way. In short, the history of accumulation exhibits successive phases, sometimes marked by a falling tendency of the rate of profit, as was the case during the "Thirty Glorious Years" of the postwar period when the working classes were benefiting from considerable political power, sometimes marked by a recovery in the rate of profit as in the decades 1980 to 2010. But then this recovery caused a problem for realization of the general supply/demand equilibrium in regard to consumer goods. The movement of this contradiction, inherent to capitalism, cannot be explained solely by the play of economic laws but by the relationship of the latter to the results of the class struggle. Bourgeois economics ignores this dialectic, to which Marx gives its proper rank.

THE QUESTION OF LAND RENTS AND
THE INTEREST ON MONEY CAPITAL

In the nineteenth century's competitive capitalism divergences between the system of values and that of prices and incomes are beyond those associated with the transformation of values into prices of production. In *Capital* Marx discusses two of those divergences, linked in one case to land rents and in the other to interest on money capital.

I have dared to call into question the economic theory of land rent, which Marx bases on the differences in organic composition of capital between agriculture and industry. Besides, Marx forgets about this theory when he shifts the emphasis of his analysis to the questions of historical materialism posed in their connection: the class conflicts and alliances linking great landowners to peasants within different forms of anti-working-class alliance.

The topic of interest raises questions relating to the functions of the monetary system and of the state, to which I will return further on.

The Twentieth Century's Initial Monopoly Capitalism (1900–1975)

Neither Marx nor even the main late-nineteenth-century Marxist thinkers believed for a moment that the system as it existed in their epoch made up a definitive structure. On the contrary, they accentuated the tendencies of its evolution ordered by the unfolding of its logic. With remarkable intuition, Marx noted the importance of the initial manifestations of the transformations in the form of capital ownership: the establishment of the first joint-stock corporations in the priority areas requiring assemblage of a large mass of capital (railroads and mines). At the time, all the Marxists predicted that forms of small commodity production would inevitably disappear and be absorbed into expanding capital. And even though the formulation of their vision of this programmed disappearance turned out to be wrong (in particular, see what Kautsky had to say about the future of agricultural production), the idea on

which their vision was based—the concentration/centralization
of capital, resulting from competition that is doomed to dialectical self-negation—was confirmed by history. So that when, at the
end of the nineteenth century, Hobson and Hilferding undertook
analyses of the new monopoly capitalism there was nothing surprising about it for the period's Marxists.

The first long systemic crisis of capitalism got under way in
the 1870s. The version of historic capitalism's extension over
the long span that I have put forward suggests a succession of
three epochs: ten centuries of incubation from the year 1000
in China to the eighteenth-century revolutions in England and
France, a short century of triumphal flourishing (the nineteenth century), probably a long decline comprising in itself
the first long crisis (1875–1945) and then the second (begun
in 1975 and still ongoing). In each of those two long crises
capital responded to the challenge by the same triple formula:
concentration of capital's control, deepening of uneven globalization, and financialization of the system's management.

Two major thinkers, Hobson and Hilferding, immediately
grasped the enormous importance of capitalism's transformation into monopoly capitalism. No surprise that the former be
British, from the nineteenth century's hegemonic power, nor
that in his analysis he would place special emphasis on the forms
of the new financialization of the system. No more surprising is
it that the latter be Austro-German, the German Empire then
being embarked on an accelerated industrialization actively supported by the state and the nascent monopolies, favored by the
large monetary indemnity imposed on France.

But it was up to Lenin to draw the political conclusion from
this transformation, which began the decline of capitalism and
thus the inscription of socialist revolution on the order of the
day. Lenin was pretty much the only one to have seen that the
powers' monopoly capitalism was pregnant with world war, the
opportunity for revolution.

The same evolution—the formation of monopoly capitalism—was under way on the other side of the Atlantic. The
Yankee victory in the Civil War had put an end to a system of
power until then largely under the sway of the South's lan-
downer/slaveowner aristocracies. And the last quarter-century's
prodigious industrial expansion was conducive to the invention
of new forms of monopoly, the only way to enable continuation
of its extension.

The primary formation of monopoly capitalism thus goes
back to the end of the nineteenth century, but in the United
States it really established itself as a system only in the 1920s, to
conquer next the Western Europe and Japan of the "Thirty Glorious Years" following the Second World War. The concept of
surplus, put forth by Paul Baran and Paul Sweezy in the 1950-60
decade, allows a grasp of what is essential in the transformation
of capitalism brought about by the dominant emergence of the
monopolies. Convinced as I was by that work of enrichment to
the Marxist critique of capitalism, I undertook as soon as the
1970s its reformulation, which required, in my opinion, the
transformation of the "first" (1920-70) monopoly capitalism
into generalized-monopoly capitalism, analyzed as a qualitatively new phase of the system.

In the previous forms of competition among firms producing
the same use value—numerous then, and independent of one
another—decisions were made by the capitalist owners of those
firms on the basis of a recognized market price that imposed
itself as an external datum. Baran and Sweezy observed that the
new monopolies acted differently: they set their prices simultaneously with the nature and volume of their outputs. So it
was an end to "fair and open competition," which remains, quite
contrary to reality, at the heart of conventional economics rhetoric. The abolition of competition, the radical transformation of
that term's meaning, of its functioning and of its results, detaches
the price system from its basis, the system of values, and in that

very way hides from sight the referential framework that used to define capitalism's rationality. Although use values once constituted to a great extent autonomous realities, they become, in monopoly capitalism, the object of actual fabrications produced systematically through aggressive and particularized sales strategies (advertising, brands, etc.).

In monopoly capitalism a coherent reproduction of the productive system is no longer possible merely by mutual adjustment of the two departments discussed in volume 2 of *Capital*: it is thenceforward necessary to take into account a Department III, conceived by Baran and Sweezy, of surplus absorption. I have tried to make an estimate of this Department III that reflects the really observed evolution of the composition of the overall output of the economies at issue over the course of the twentieth century. I thus refer the reader to that illustration of the modus operandi of monopoly capitalism, which a reading of Baran and Sweezy inspired me to write (see Part Two).

The excrescence of Department III, in turn, favors, in fact, the erasure of the distinction made by Marx between productive labor-producing surplus value and not productive labor. All forms of wage labor can become, and do become, sources of possible profits. A hairdresser sells his services to a customer who pays him out of his income. But if that hairdresser becomes the employee of a beauty parlor, the business must realize a profit for its owner. Exploited labor is no longer only that of the producers of surplus value, as I recalled in the comments I put forth regarding the patchwork makeup of Department III. If the country at issue puts ten million wage workers to work in Departments I, II, and III, providing the equivalent of twelve million years of abstract labor, and if the wages received by those workers allow them to buy goods and services requiring merely six million years of abstract labor, the rate of exploitation for all of them, productive and unproductive confounded, is the same 100 percent. But the six million years of abstract labor that the workers do not receive cannot all be invested in the purchase of producer goods destined to the expansion of Departments I and II; part of them will have to be put toward the expansion of Department III.

GENERALIZED MONOPOLY CAPITALISM SINCE 1975

Passage from initial monopoly capitalism to its current form (generalized-monopoly capitalism) was accomplished in a short time (between 1975 and 2000) in response to the second long crisis of declining capitalism. In fifteen years, monopoly power's centralization and its capacity for control over the entire productive system reached summits incomparable with what had until then been the case.

My first formulation of generalized-monopoly capitalism dates from 1978, when I put forward an interpretation of capital's responses to the challenge of its long systemic crisis, which opened starting in 1971 to 1975. In that interpretation I accentuated the three directions of this expected response, then barely under way: strengthened centralization of control over the economy by the monopolies, deepening of globalization (and the outsourcing of manufacturing industry toward the peripheries), and financialization. The work that André Gunder Frank and I published together in 1978 drew no notice, probably because our theses were ahead of their time. But today the three characteristics at issue have become blindingly obvious to everybody.[1]

A name had to be given to this new phase of monopoly capitalism. "Late monopoly capitalism"? I thought that the adjective "late," sort of like the prefix "post," ought to be avoided because by itself it gives no positive indication about the content and full significance of the novel features. The adjective "generalized" specifies this: the monopolies are thenceforward in a position giving them the capability of reducing all (or nearly all) economic activities to subcontractor status. The example of family farming in the capitalist centers provides the finest example of this.

These farmers are controlled upstream by the monopolies that provide their inputs and financing, downstream by the marketing chains, to the point that the price structures forced on them wipe out the income from their labor. Farmers only survive thanks to public subsidies paid for by the taxpayers. This extraction is thus at the origin of the monopolies' profits. As has been observed likewise with bank failures, the new principle of economic management is summed up in a phrase: privatization of the monopolies' profits, socialization of their losses. To go on talking of "fair and open competition" and of "truth of the prices revealed by the markets" belongs in a farce. But economists have no sense of humor, and the persistence they show in carrying on the study of an imaginary system that has nothing to do with reality qualifies them for the Nobel Prizes handed out to them!

The fragmented, and by that fact concrete, economic power of proprietary bourgeois families gives way to a centralized power exercised by the directors of the monopolies and their cohort of salaried servitors. For generalized-monopoly capitalism involves not the concentration of property, which on the contrary is more dispersed than ever, but the power to manage it. That is why it is deceptive to attach the adjective "patrimonial" to contemporary capitalism. It is only in appearance that shareholders rule. Absolute monarchs, the top executives of the monopolies decide everything in their name. In turn, that management wipes out the former modus operandi of competition among capitals, which used to constitute the basis for the way in which capital accumulation was regulated. It puts in its place a way of management based on alternation between negotiated cooperation and brutal competition among monopolies (which works through methods that are not those of the "fair and open competition" in which we are supposed to believe). Power, in the most abstract sense of the term, takes the place of concrete effective competition. Moreover, the deepening globalization of the system wipes out the holistic—that is, simultaneously economic, political, and social—logic of national systems without putting in its place any global logic whatsoever. This is the "empire of chaos" (title of one of my works, published in 1991, and subsequently taken up by others). In fact international political violence takes the place of economic competition, while the discourse seeks to make us believe that regulation of the system results from this.[2]

The New System: Prices and Incomes Disconnected from Values

The concept of generalized-monopoly capitalism allows us to locate the significance of the major transformations involving the configuration of class structures and the ways in which political life is managed in the centers and in the peripheries.

In the system's centers (the Triad of United States, Western Europe, and Japan), generalized-monopoly capitalism has brought with it generalization of the wage form. The so-called upper managers, linked to management of the economy by the monopolies, are thenceforward employees who do not participate in the formation of surplus value, of which they have become consumers, deserving by that fact to be characterized as a component sector of the bourgeoisie. At the other social pole, the generalized proletarianization that the wage form suggests is accompanied by a multiplication in the forms of segmentation of the labor force. In other words, the proletariat, in its forms as known in the past, disappears at the very moment when proletarianization becomes generalized.

In the peripheries—as always extremely diverse since they are only defined negatively, as regions that have not become established as centers of the global system—the (direct or indirect)

effects of domination by generalized-monopoly capital are no less
visible. Above the diversity both of local ruling classes and statuses
of subordinate classes is the power of a dominant super-class emerging in the wake of globalization. This super-class is sometimes
that of "comprador insiders," sometimes that of the governing political class (or class-state-party), or a mixture of the two.

The power of domination of the economy by generalized-monopoly capitalism has required and made possible the
transformation of the forms in which political life is managed. In
the centers, a new political consensus culture synonymous with
depoliticization, has taken the place of the political culture based
on the right-left confrontation that used to give significance
to bourgeois democracy and the contradictory inscription of
class struggles within its framework. Far from being synonyms,
"market," that is, the "non-market" that char-acterizes management of the economy by the generalized monopolies, and
"democracy" are antonyms. In the peripheries, the monopoly of
power captured by the dominant local super-class, which I refer
to in my 2013 book, *The Implosion of Contemporary Capitalism*,
likewise involves the negation of democracy.[3] This, in turn, for-
tifies forms of depolitization, forms that are diverse but whose
effects are quite the same. I have tried to provide an example
appropriate to those countries that are victims of the rise of political Islam.

Domination by the capital of the generalized monopolies is
exercised on the world scale through global integration of the
monetary and financial market, based on the principle of flexible
exchange rates, abandonment of the gold standard, and giving up
national controls over the flow of capital. Nevertheless, this domination is called into question, to varying degrees, by state policies
of the emerging countries. The conflict between these policies
and the strategic objectives of the Triad's collective imperialism
becomes by that fact one of the central axes for possibly putting
generalized-monopoly capitalism once more on trial.

The new financialization of economic life crowns this transformation in capital's power. In place of the concrete forms of
its expression is abstract affirmation of the power of capital. Instead of strategies set out by real owners of fragmented capital,
we have those of the managers of ownership titles over capital.
What is vulgarly called fictitious capital (the estimated value of
ownership certificates) is nothing but the expression of this dis-
placement, this disconnect between the virtual and real worlds.

The abstract character of contemporary capital is synonymous with permanent, insurmountable, chaos. By its very
nature capitalist accumulation has always been synonymous
with disorder, in the sense that Marx gave to that term: a system
moving from disequilibrium to disequilibrium, driven by class
struggles and conflicts among the Powers, without ever tending
toward an equilibrium. But this disorder resulting from competition among fragmented capitals was kept within reasonable
limits through management of the credit system carried out
under the control of the national state. With abstract contemporary capitalism, those frontiers disappear; the violence of the
movements from disequilibrium to disequilibrium is reinforced.
The successor of disorder is chaos.

Bourgeois economic theory endeavors to try to answer the
challenge of chaos by denying its existence. To do that, it continues its conventional discourse, which talks of "fair and open
competition," nonexistent in fact, and of "true prices." One talks
of "less state" although the public-sector share of GDP not only
never has been so large but also constitutes the condition *sine
qua non* for survival of the system! But in parallel to this empty
and unreal discourse, the theory claims to reconstruct the (false)
theorem of market self-regulation by shifting the analysis of economic decision making, attributed without proof to individuals,
to their expectations. Thus the circle is closed: economic theory,
still that of an imaginary system (and not that of real capitalism)
is, to boot, one enabling foresight of anything and everything as

a function of expectations whose conformity to reality remains forever unknown. Economic theory is, more than ever, an ideological discourse, in the most negative sense of the term, aimed at forcing acceptance of decisions made by the only deciders: the generalized monopolies.

REGULATION OF CAPITALISM BY THE STATE
AND THE CREDIT SYSTEM

Struggles and alliances among classes, competition among capitals, and conflicts among the powers—realities that all belong to the domain of historical materialism and for that reason cannot be reduced to workings of economic law as suggested by conventional economics—thus result in a system that moves from disequilibrium to disequilibrium without ever tending toward an equilibrium that can in advance be defined in economic terms. By nature, capitalism is an unstable system. Thus the disorder that characterizes it is a reality that cannot be gotten rid of by any economistic reduction.

This disorder, nevertheless, is successfully regulated, often (but not always) by national state policies mobilizing, on one hand, the systematic construction of hegemonic social blocs, and on the other, national management of the system of money and of credit. State and money together make up the means utilized to overcome the disorder resulting from the conflicts of interest among capitals, that is, capital whose ownership is segmented. The state thus often acts "against" the interests of capitalists at odds with one another, in order that the interests of capitalism prevail.

This way of regulation was based, in the nineteenth century, on adoption of metal as a money commodity, with bimetallism evolving toward gold monometallism. This system rules out the possibility of financing inflation through uncontrolled credit expansion. To this end, I distinguish the large waves of price change linked to those ordering gold production from true inflation, which is a subsequent phenomenon. In this connection I have adopted Marx's analyses concerning the relations between gold production and the demand for money; I have extended his arguments by my proposition of an "active role of credit" in accumulation as an answer to Rosa Luxemburg's observations on the realization of surplus value. Here I refer the reader to my book: *Unequal Development*.[4]

It is indeed quite possible to compute the amount of credit that must of necessity be advanced to capitalists at the start of each production cycle for surplus value to be realized and the loans repaid at the end of the cycle. The rate of growth of this amount of credit is itself calculable; it is a function of the rate of growth of GDP and the growth rates of productivity in each of the Departments I and II. This reckoning gives objective status to the concept of demand for money called on by Marx against quantity theories of money. It gives its full meaning to Marx's affirmation that demand for money creates its supply. The possible effectiveness of the credit system is thus not a stylistic approximation but a concrete precise reality that I have termed "the active function of money in accumulation." The proposed method, derived from Marx's reproduction schemata in *Capital*, volume 2, makes explicit that which Marx had left vague and uncalculated. Unfortunately, Marxists are too often content with nothing more than doing exegeses of Marx. By that they have even weakened his argument, which, extended as I do, annihilates the validity of any monetarist theory, previous or contemporary.

The efficacity of the credit system, its capacity to fulfill correctly the requirements of accumulation, obviously depends on conditions that have to be specified. This policy can be, and generally was, efficacious as long as it was working within the framework of a self-centered national productive system. And, in that sense, money and state are inseparable, which was the case until the 1970s. It is no longer so since the national state gave up fulfilling its role in regulating accumulation by regulating credit, without a supranational state taking up the task, and since, in parallel, national management of the monetary system gave way to the vagaries of a globalized and integrated monetary and financial system. This setting adrift, forced by the generalized monopolies raising themselves to the rank of sole actor, led me to conclude that we are dealing with an unviable, naturally chaotic system. The deviation involves not only the global system; in the same way, it involves the European subsystem and that of the euro, based on the same principles. The ongoing implosion of the euro stands witness to that.

The new strategy of the dominant monopoly-capitalist firms was scarcely reconcilable with nineteenth-century techniques of managing capitalism, based on the gold standard system.

Also, the disappearance from sight of the fundamental reference points established by values was concomitant with the progressive abandonment of historic capitalism's other solid point of reference—commodity money (metal, gold)—an abandonment started by the chaos of the First World War. The attempt to return to gold during the interwar period malfunctioned. The solution provided by the Bretton Woods system (1945–71) was effective only insofar as the United States by itself took on the functions of the hegemonic economy (the dollar-based gold exchange standard), and it disappeared in 1971 when the international convertibility of the dollar into gold was terminated. Since then, floating exchange rates have introduced yet another ground for permanent chaos.

The loss of the reference point constituted by metallic money implies a critique of the logic of accumulation. That loss of reference brought about the appearance of a new way to manage accumulation, linked to the disorder of thenceforward possible inflation. Currently, the affirmed will to preclude any inflationary outlook, still without a return to metallic money but by carrying out permanent deflationary monetary policies (a will affirmed more by Germany than by others) calls for a reconsideration and deepening of the concept of money in capitalism. Losing sight of the solid reference point of metallic money might have been compensated for by centralized management of credit, carried out by the state. In part, this solution was utilized throughout the thirty "glorious" postwar years. The system's entry, starting in 1975, into crisis and the response given in terms of deepening globalization (and for Europe a construction inscribed into the globalization at issue) led the state to abandon this management of credit and to yield it to the monopolies' direct power. But the resulting stagnation and chaos have put the gold fetish back in the saddle, showing in this way the inseparability of economistic alienation from the permanence of an indispensable fetish.

National methods of regulating competitive capitalism, and even monopoly capitalism in its primary form, were effective, and were expressed in the succession of expansionary phases and of phases of readjustment via crisis that make up the economic cycle.

Living and Dead Labor, the Time Factor, Discounting the Future, and the Rate of Interest

The law of value involves the possibility of summing quantities of living and of dead labor. Bourgeois economics deals with this matter by introducing time into its argument: capital equipment is first produced, then used. This, of course, is obvious. But behind this treatment can be seen an ethical a priori: saving must first occur before there can be investment. And as long as this is so, the income on capital (equated to capital equipment) finds its justification in the sacrifice represented by saving, a sacrifice defined by the price of time, which is termed discount of the future. The triteness of the argument stems from an identification between individual behavior and the reality of social function. An individual with foresight saves first, invests next. Puritan morality shines through the praise of such behavior. It is next transposed to the collectivity: the nation must save in order to invest. Politicians, right-wingers and social democrats alike, repeat it in accord with one another.

Now, at the scale of the reality of the capitalist mode of production, things do not happen that way. The production of means of production and means of consumption is concomitant, it orders a social division of labor between Departments I and II. Expanded reproduction involves Department I producing a surplus beyond mere replacement of depreciated equipment. Time is indeed taken into account, since that surplus will be used in the next phase of production, but not in the way it is in the puritan argument referred to above. For it is the decision to invest (to have Department I produce more than needed to cover depreciation) that creates saving, which does not precede investment but follows from it. Keynes as well as Marx recognized the fallacy involved in treating individual (micro) behavior as the same as social (macro) behavior.

Here again, the contrast between the system's claimed absolute rationality and its necessary relativization shows itself in full daylight. Investment decisions are not taken collectively; they result from competition that forces firms to plan their modernization and expansion, thus creating a potential demand for capital equipment exceeding the requirements of depreciation. Expanded reproduction results from the rationality of the system, which seems absolute. Raised to the higher level, represented by society (which is not to be reduced to the entrepreneurial class), the rationality of investment decisions ought to be ordered according to other criteria, relativizing the criteria ordering capitalist reproduction. Considerations about the use of natural resources, which we will come to further on, will have to find their place identified among those criteria, though they are ignored by the falsely absolute rationality of bourgeois economics. In the same way, from a social point of view, the generations of youth in training, of active workers, and of pensioners must be considered as solidary elements composing the same society and not as entities competing with one another.

How Does Marx Take Account of Time in Economic Calculation?

Bourgeois economics treats the rate by which the future is discounted as a component of the interest rate, which is also and simultaneously the price paid for acquiring the advantage of liquidity. The rate of profit—itself the sum of the rate of interest and a supposed "risk premium"—is by that very fact defined in temporal terms: the annual profit returned by capital.

With a clear conscience Marx ignores the concept of discounting the future. He puts forth his own treatment of interest in the framework of the redistribution of surplus value. Nevertheless, Marx integrates time into his analysis of capitalist economic calculation, whose logic, that of a system guided by maximization of capital's annual rate of profit, he carefully restores. The times needed for production, for the circulation of capital, and for the realization of the product undergo a constant pressure tending toward their reduction. The procedures put into operation with this in mind produce effects of redistribution of surplus value in the course of its transformation into profit.

But what of longer time spans? Here we again come upon the challenges of social rationalities transcending those of capitalist management. Among others, precisely, are those of dealing with the "long or very long-term" effects of the choices of social logic.

In times to come, we will perhaps conceive an "appreciation of the future" rather than its discounting.

AT THE BORDERS OF THE CAPITALIST
MODE OF PRODUCTION

Marx, who carried out his research by starting from the visible concrete and rising to the level of the abstract, proceeds in the opposite direction to present their results. Thus *Capital* begins with an exposition of the essence of the mode of production grasped at the highest level of abstraction, which can be termed "pure capitalism," reduced to two classes and a single mode of labor—wage labor. In the system of capitalist production, taken at that level of abstraction, Marx's distinction between productive labor, paid out of variable capital, and unproductive labor, paid for by the spending of income, takes on great importance: productive labor is termed such because it alone produces surplus value. In contrast, the work of state employees, providers of public services, like that of private providers of services paid for out of personal incomes, has no part in the extraction of surplus-value—it provides for its redistribution.

But obviously the real concrete capitalist society—the capitalist formations—can never be reduced to a "pure" mode of production. And when Marx comes down to the concrete, it was obviously to what was concrete in his epoch. In the nineteenth century capitalist production relations occupied a limited space in the totality of production relations: the domains ruled by peasant and artisanal production still take up a large part of the terrain, and preserve a measure of still-active effective autonomy even as their subordination to the dominant logics of capital accumulation continually increase.

The importance of this observation stems from the fact that the expansion of capitalist relations will take place in the

nineteenth century precisely through the destruction or absorption, or formal subordination, of the earlier forms, a process that
gives to the capitalism of the epoch its triumphant character
synonymous with progress, as the sentences of the *Communist
Manifesto* bear witness. And it is for this reason that I have given
a reading of the expansion of capitalism that reduces the progressive phase of the system to that short nineteenth century. Rosa
Luxemburg had given proof of a fine intuition when she insisted
on the importance for expanded reproduction of the absorption
or subordination of non-capitalist forms of production. Her
arguments about the role of imperialist capitalism's expansion in
the colonies and semi-colonies of the fin de siècle can be transferred, mutatis mutandis, to the conditions of capital's internal
expansion in the countries of Europe between 1830 and 1880.
My critique bears on a different aspect of Rosa Luxemburg's
thesis, which has to do with the supposed impossibility of reali-
zing surplus-value in a model of pure capitalism, which I refute
through my propositions regarding the active role of credit in the
accumulation process.

Things have changed greatly since then. Monopoly capitalism
brings with it accelerated generalization of the waged form of labor,
so much so that in the United States the crisis of 1930 breaks out in
an almost completely wage-earning society. Thence its novel character. And my reading of this first long systemic crisis, then, sees
it as the first wave in the decline of capitalism. With generalized
monopoly, capitalism completes the process of integration and
subordination of the productive system in its entirety. Contemporary capitalism then seeks to overcome its crisis through a new
expansion of the field of social activities subordinated to the logic
of profit extraction by privatizing public services (the common
property) and by inventing a new field of business—the environ-
mental domain, about which I will have more to say.

Marx was right to specify which boundaries of social labor
are to be taken into account at each stage of development, and to

distinguish between the social labor proper to capitalism and the other forms of labor being carried out in spaces not governed (or not yet governed) by capitalist relations. To call these forms "not socially useful" (for capital) is both true and false. On the one hand, these areas of reality evade direct domination by capital, but on the other, their very existence affects the reproduction conditions of social labor under direct domination of capital.

Feminism made broad contributions to the thought process that allowed full daylight to be thrown onto these "clandestine" relations. For the "free" labor of women in the household framework enables reduction of the real wages paid to those workers selling their labor power. Once again the social space administered by capital cannot be separated from its environment (other social spaces located outside that controlled directly by capital). Once more capitalism's rationality loses its absolute character and becomes relative in the vaster social space surrounding and transcending it. On that vaster scale this rationality even turns into irrationality; for on that scale rationality is inseparable from human emancipation, which involves trespassing beyond mercantile alienation.

Women's labor is not the sole example of these forms working outside the narrow field of capital's direct domination. As soon as one steps outside the restricted field of the capitalist mode of production (the two departments), one is confronted, in the social formations of really existing capital-ism, with apparently "independent" forms of labor (like the labor of peasant producers) that in reality are integrated and subordinated (though indirectly) to capital's exploitation, as has already been seen. Inflating Department III with surplus absorption likewise offers new possibilities for expanding the field of operation of capitalist relations. This transformation of capitalism deprives the distinction between productive and unproductive labor of its central place insofar as the waged forms of unproductive labor become a source for the extraction of profits.

Social labor in Marx is always labor operating on the basis of scientific and technical knowledge (every mode of production is "cognitive"; for that reason Marx speaks of a general intellect inseparable from the productivity of social labor), and in a given framework of natural conditions. The problem is, then, to know whether the availability of natural resources is to be viewed as part of the capitalist mode or as located at its boundary.

In this regard, bourgeois economics considers only natural resources fallen into private ownership and thereby having a price. It deals with them as constitutive elements of cost, as factors of production in their own right. So be it. But then it ignores two sets of serious problems: the possible exhaustion of certain resources and the overall effects of their utilization. These are two sets of problems rediscovered by contemporary environmentalism.

Is the "social price" paid through exhaustion a "just" price because it is defined by the supply price of the owners of exhaustible resources? Certainly not, above all when national considerations are reintroduced into the reality of really existing globalized capitalism: the inequality crystallized in the trading of nonrenewable resources for renewable commodities.

Bourgeois economics proposes, to deal with unowned, "free" resources, consideration of the "external economies" involved in access to their utilization. Beyond the difficulties in measuring the former—always mostly artificial—it is hard to see how really existing capitalism might let its functioning be subordinated to their requirements.

Marx does not ignore the problem. He discusses the subject in distinguishing "wealth" from "value." Value is the exclusive product of social labor, socially organized on the basis of capitalist relations. But Marx does not say that wealth is the exclusive product of social labor. He says that the latter is the combined result of the former and of "nature." Private appropriation of certain means of accessing what it offers, especially in regard to the soil, gives under capitalism a "right" to part of the produced value. This is how Marx treats the subject of ground rent. So I am always surprised by the confusions sustained about this by some contemporary Marxists who talk indistinguishably about "wealth" and "value."

On this question I have developed the thesis that capitalism is by its very nature unable to take into account that requirement, which transcends it. But what, then, to put in place of the narrow criteria of capitalist rationality? Knowing that the operation of those criteria strengthens the increasingly destructive side of capitalist accumulation and that, because of this, capitalist economic rationality is social irrationality on the scale of the human race. Marx knew this, said so, but put forward no positive alternative. We know his critique of "utopian socialisms" and his refusal to "give recipes for the cookpots of the future." He leaves to the materialist dialectic the task of settling this future problem, through consciousness and the social class struggle. I share this viewpoint, which does not exclude, but includes, the need to give to critical utopia's fantasies the role that they deserve in building the alternative: twenty-first-century socialism.

Is there any use to our arguments going outside the narrow framework of the capitalist mode? I answer in the affirmative because it is precisely by this means that one can put one's finger on the limits of capitalism's rationality, that one can reveal the conflict pitting its rationality against the higher rationality inseparable from human emancipation. Thus, for example, beyond the concrete political analysis of the composition of the content of the portmanteau represented by Department III, it is necessary to identify those of its elements that though rational from the point of view of capital appreciation are irrational from the point of view of emancipation.

Once again the future, beyond capitalism, is there to build. But it is useful, on this plane as on others, to leave to the creative

fantasy of utopia the breathing space allowing it to propose and
to act toward building the emancipatory alternative.

THE SOCIAL POWER OF CAPITAL

The characteristics of historic capitalism are at the origin of
a confusion between the concept of capital and the concrete
reality in which it is embodied—producer goods. Bourgeois
economics is responsible for this confusion and confesses to it
through its claim to discover the specific productivity tied to
the utilization of production instruments. Marx is never guilty
of this confusion. His concept of capital sees it as a social relationship of production enabling the extraction of surplus value;
and the capital that a capitalist must gather to enable this is not
limited to the fraction of capital destined for the purchase of production instruments (constant capital) but equally includes that
intended for the payment of wages (variable capital).

Social power is a concept that must be handled with great
care, for the social power of capital is exercised in a specific way,
different from how power was exercised in former societies.
With capitalism we are present at a reversal of the ordering of
political and economic factors. In the societies that preceded
capitalist modernity, the political factor is dominant and the
economic subordinate to it. In capitalism, for the first time in
history, the economic factor becomes directly dominant. Put
crudely, before capitalism power is the source of wealth, in capitalism wealth becomes the source of power. This reversal is at the
origin of the emergence of economic science, which claims to
discover the laws governing economic life independently from
the vicissitudes of politics, in this way dissociating economics
from politics.

The forms in which capital exerts its power have, in turn,
undergone transformations paralleling the transformation from

capitalism into monopoly, and then generalized-monopoly capitalism. In the nineteenth century the power of capital was exercised
through the concrete procedures of the epoch's social struggles.
This power was in the first place that of the business owners who
hire the wage-workers. It must be said: capital employs (and
exploits) the workers; it is not the case that the workers simply
make use of the means of production. Next, this power is the
result of the ability of this new bourgeois class to negotiate a sharing of general (political and economic) power with other social
classes—the former aristocracies, the peasantry, or, later and only
in part, the working class. The power of the general-ized monopolies grows to a new size and exalts itself into a new, exclusive and
absolute centralized power. This transformation is accompanied
by transformation of the system of prices and incomes that casts
aside all reference to values and to surplus-value. The conditions
are then brought together so that the immediate reality—the
structure of prices and incomes—resulting from society's adjustment to the monopolies' strategies, is alone on stage. One thus has
the illusion that capital is no longer anything but the expression
of a pure power, that of capital. We have thus reached the deepest
level of mercantile alienation, the violence of whose expression is
increased yet more by financialization.

THE GLOBALIZATION OF VALUE

The transformation of values into globalized values constitutes a
major dimension of the political economy of modern times. Each
stage in the development of historic capitalism corresponded
to specific forms of this transformation, an analysis of which
has been at the center in many of my major works. That is why I
content myself here referring the reader to Part One of this book
and to the chapter devoted to the international economy in *Unequal Development*. Marx had aimed to write a chapter of *Capital*

devoted to international trade, which never saw daylight. My critique of economic theories about movements in the balance of foreign payments led me to move the discussion to the domain of historical materialism and to conclude that the peripheries were subordinated to unilateral and permanent structural adjustment, shaping their structures in conformity with the requirements of accumulation in the dominant centers.

As far as this synthetic essay is concerned, I will only say that in Marx's epoch the page of the first world system—the mercantilist system—already belongs to the past, although that of the formation of the new imperialist is still to be written. China, the Ottoman Empire, Sub-Saharian Africa generally remain external to the new globalized capitalism a-birthing. Nevertheless, the major British colonial heritage—India—holds a crucial place in it; and it is this domination and not its supposed industrial progress that gave Great Britain its hegemonic position in the nineteenth century.

Struggles and alliances among classes, competition among capitals, and conflicts among powers—realities all pertaining to the domain of historical materialism, and thereby not reducible to economic laws as conventional economics suggests—result in a system that wanders from disequilibrium to disequilibrium without ever tending toward the realization of an equilibrium that could be predefined in economic terms. Capitalism is, by nature, an unstable system. Its characteristic disorder is thus a reality that no economistic reduction can get rid of. But, of course, national regulation is not everything. It is constrained to enlist in the epoch's globalization, itself modeled on conflict among the powers. Once again, the latter is not reducible to some economic competitiveness that could be dissociated from the effects of internal social struggles and of international political and military conflicts.

That whole system of the nineteenth century was thus in movement, and the direction of this movement can be seen: it led to the concentration/centralization of capital. The monopoly capitalism that was to be born from this movement then calls back into question the activity of the ensemble of forces that brought to pass the divergences between the system of values and that of prices and incomes, alike at national levels and at that of globalized capitalism.

Beyond Capitalism: A Look Back at the Concept of Social Value

I have wished, in presenting this synthesis, to take up again the conclusions I had reached in my previous works concerning the analysis of the causes, the directions, and the bearing of the divergences between the system of values and that of prices and incomes such as it was in nineteenth-century competitive capitalism and such as it has become in the contemporary epoch of generalized-monopoly capitalism. This evolution is that of a system that has raised itself above concrete forms of the manifestations of the social power of capital all the way to the final abstract form through which it would express itself henceforward.

The objective of this labor was simply to analyze the reality of contemporary generalized-monopoly capitalism, and, in that way demonstrate that this system is not viable and that its implosion, already ongoing, is inevitable. In this sense contemporary capitalism deserves the adjective "senile" that I have applied to it: the autumn of capitalism. I did not want to go further and put forward political action strategies enabling construction of a positive alternative. To take up that challenge would have required study of fundamental questions that are not touched on, in particular that of active social subjects. Elsewhere I had sketched out the broad outlines of the challenges, which, according to me, cannot be taken up except on condition that bold, radical-leftist movements are recomposed. Then and only then can the autumn of capitalism and the springtime of the peoples coincide. This is not yet the case. The only thing I ascertain is the expected implosion of the system. This is accompanied then by revolts of the southern peoples, the rise of conflicts between the emergent countries and the centers of the historic imperialist Triad, the implosion of the European system, and the rise of new struggles in the centers themselves. All that augurs well for the possibility of radical leftist movements, up to the challenges, being reborn.

The preceding elaborations help answer the question before us: has the progression in the productivity of social labor, arising in the framework of capitalist expansion, brought about "social progress" in a broader, yet to be specified, sense?

The extension of capitalism is ordered by the capitalist law of transformed value, which governs not merely expanded reproduction but, in short, all aspects of social life, which it subordinates to the prioritized requirements of capital appreciation. There is no "market economy," to use the banal fashionable terminology, which does not result in a "market society." The rationality of economic decision making showcased by the bourgeois economists is a relative rationality, that is, irrationality when raised from the level of economic management to that of the entire scope of social life.

The progression of productive forces linked to the unfolding of this logic is not synonymous with unqualified progress. For it has, and always has had, simultaneous constructive and destructive effects. This contradiction, immanent in the materialist dialectic of capitalist extension, worsens to the exact extent that history moves forward in the framework of this system. It has now reached such a point that henceforward the destructive aspects of capitalism can be said to prevail broadly over its progressive contributions. Contemporary environmentalism rightly accentuates this overturn. For my part, I have accentuated a different dimension of the contradiction:

the increasing divergence between the material conditions available to majorities in the centers and to those in the peripheries of the global capitalist system, which is the main form of the pauperization that Marx, rightly, linked to the unfolding of the capital/labor contradiction.

Marx's fundamental methodological instrument, the materialist dialectic, had already enabled him to grasp entirely the ambivalence of progress achieved by and within capitalism. Marx says of this mode of production that, with increasing force, it destroys, in step with its expansion, the very foundations of society: "man" (the alienated and exploited workers) and "nature." Thence, Marx concluded, the capitalist system could constitute only one stage in history. The idea that it might be "the end of history" as is said nowadays, or, a bit more elegantly, that it is a system capable of unlimited adaptation to the requirements of change, is scarcely anything but nonsense. Capitalism has adapted, and can still adapt, to many requirements but never those that are essential to the overcoming of its fundamental contradiction. But Marx did not draw from this the conclusion that socialism, defined as a higher, emancipation-based stage in the unfolding of human civilization, was "inevitable." The method of the materialist dialectic forbade that to him. Marx had an open, even though optimistic, vision of the future. He did not exclude "self-destruction," to which he actually referred explicitly. Of course, the Soviet vulgarization that passed for Marxism had declared socialism to be "inevitable." Doing so, it put in place of the materialist dialectic operative in Marx's historical materialism a mechanistic interpretation in which supposed "laws" make up a closed and finished theory of history.

So the question of the future is still open. But we must prepare it, contribute to evolution going toward transcendence of capitalism by building the socialist alternative, and lessen the risks of a self-destructive shipwreck. How are we to prepare that better future based on reason and human emancipation (themselves inseparable)? Marx had put class struggle led by the working class (the proletariat) at the center of his answer to the question. He explicitly said that the coming socialism would be the result of that struggle, and refused to define its content "in advance" too specifically. The method guiding this strategic choice of action—"it is not merely a matter of understanding the world, but of changing it"—is, in my opinion, still valid, on condition that the narrow concept of "working class," tacitly understood as being that of the advanced industrialized countries, be replaced with the much broader totality of lower classes and of dominated and exploited peoples. This would take account of the reality represented by the polarization linked to really existing capitalism's globalized expansion.

Socialism, a stage or series of stages on the long road to communism conceived as a higher phase of human civilization, will certainly have to develop strategies progressively reducing, and finally abolishing, the reign of the capitalist law of transformed value. But what of social value and of the productivity of social labor?

The concept of social value lights our lamp and calls on us to conceive what the construction requirements of the socialism to come are, of an economic management based on the social utility of those goods and services that society in its totality (not the capitalists) decides to produce. It provides us not with a ready-to-be-applied recipe but merely with a principle: fusion between economic and political management and their common subordination to the workings of the egalitarian democracy of all individuals, simultaneously citizens, producers, and consumers, from schoolchildren to pensioners. The consciousness of this necessity is evident: "civilization's discontents" (to pick up Freud's phrase, but giving it a different meaning) are already felt forcibly by all the peoples of the contemporary world.

The propositions for an action strategy to that end, which I have raised in my book *The Implosion of Contemporary Capitalism*, are placed in this perspective of contribution to the rebirth of the radical left, that is to say, radical in its critique of capitalism, whose formulation Marx had begun but in no way completed.

CHAPTER EIGHT

The Surplus in Monopoly Capitalism and the Imperialist Rent

Paul Baran and Paul Sweezy dared, and were able, to continue the work begun by Marx. Starting from the observation that capitalism's inherent tendency was to allow increases in the value of labor power (wages) only at a rate lower than the rate of increase in the productivity of social labor, they deduced that the disequilibrium resulting from this distortion would lead to stagnation absent systematic organization of ways to absorb the excess profits stemming from that tendency.

This observation was the starting point for the definition they gave to the new concept of "surplus." Baran then extended Marx's analysis of the dynamic of capital accumulation in volume two of *Capital*, restricted to a system reduced to the two Departments of Production of means of production and of consumption goods respectively, with the introduction of a surplus-absorbing Department III.

I have always considered this bold stroke as a crucial contribution to the creative utilization of Marx's thoughts. Baran and Sweezy dared and were able to "start from Marx," but they

refused to stop, like so many other Marxists, at the exegesis of
his writings.

Having, for my part, completely accepted this crucial contribution from Baran and Sweezy, I would like, in this modest
offering devoted to honoring their work, to put forward a "quantitative metric" of that surplus.

METRIC OF THE SURPLUS

The surplus at issue, then, is the result of growth in the productivity of social labor exceeding the price paid for labor power.
Let us assume, for example, that the rate of growth in the
productivity of social labor is about 4.5 percent per year, sufficient to double the net product over a period of about fifteen
years, corresponding to an assumed average lifetime for capital
equipment. Department I consists of investment goods, which
equal invested profits, and Department II consists of wage
goods, which equal wages. To simplify the argument, we will
assume that for both departments the organic compositions of
capital and the rates of growth of labor productivity are fixed.
To permit changes in those parameters would force us to use
algebraic notation for the model, which might easily be done
but could make it harder for non-mathematicians to understand. Taking those complications into account would change
less than the net product.

So let us assume that, in the long run, real wages would grow
at a rate of about 2.5 percent per year to bring about an increase
of 40 percent over a fifteen-year span. We end up with changes in
the key magnitudes of the model in conformity with the above
table (numbers approximated).

At the end of a half-century's regular and continuous evolution of the system, the surplus, which defines the size of
Department III relative to net revenue, itself the sum of wages,

Year	Net Revenue	Dept. I	Dept. II	Dept. III
1	100	50	50	0
15	200	70	70	60
30	400	100	100	200
45	800	140	140	520

reinvested profits, and surplus, takes up two-thirds of the net product (roughly equivalent to GDP).[5]

The shift indicated is approximately what happened during the twentieth century in the "developed" centers of world capitalism (the United States/Europe/Japan Triad). Keynes had indeed noted that mature capitalism was stricken by a latent tendency toward persistent stagnation. But he had not explained that tendency, which would have required him to seriously take into account the replacement of the "classical" competitive model by monopoly capitalism. His explanation thus remained tautological: stagnation was the result of the—unexplained—fall in the marginal efficiency of capital or expected profits on new investment (below even the strongest liquidity preference). In contrast, Baran and Sweezy explained to perfection both the tendency toward stagnation and the means used to overcome it. They unraveled the mysteries of contemporary capitalism.

Initially—that is, until the 1914 war—surplus amounted in practice merely to tax-financed state expenditures of at most 10 to 15 percent of GDP. It was a matter of spending to maintain the sovereign (public administration, police, armed forces), of expenditures linked to the public management of some social services (education and public health), and of the installation of some infrastructural elements (roads and bridges, ports, railroad lines). Analysis of the components corresponding to the concept of surplus shows the diversity of the regulations governing their administration.

Corresponding approximately to Marx's Departments I and II in the national accounts are the sectors defined respectively as "primary" (agricultural production and mining), "secondary" (manufacturing), and a portion of so-called tertiary activities that is hard to derive from statistics not designed for that purpose, even when the definition of their status is not itself confusing. To be held to participate—indirectly—in the output of Departments I and II are transportation of implements, raw materials, and finished products; trade in those products; and the cost of managing the financial institutions needed to service the two departments. What are not to be regarded as direct or indirect constitutive elements in their output, and therefore counted as elements of surplus, are government administration, public expenditures and transfer payments (for education, health, social security, pensions, and old-age benefits), services (advertising) corresponding to selling costs, and personal services paid for from income (including housing).

Whether the "services" at issue, lumped together in the national accounts under the title "tertiary activities" (with the possibility of distinguishing among them a new sector termed quaternary), are administered by public or private entities does not by itself qualify them as belonging to Department III (the surplus). The fact remains that the volume of "tertiary" activities in the developed countries of the center (and also in many of the peripheral countries, though that question—a different one—does not concern us here) is much larger than that of the primary and secondary sector. Moreover, the sum of taxes and obligatory contributions in those countries by itself amounts to or exceeds 40 percent of their GDP. Talk by some fundamentalist right-wing ideologists calling for "reduction" of these fiscal extractions is purely demagogic: capitalism can no longer function in any other way. In reality, any possible decrease in the taxes paid by the "rich" must necessarily be made up by heavier taxation on the "poor."

We can thus estimate without risk of major error that the

"surplus" (Department III) accounts for half of GDP or, in other terms, has grown from 10 percent of GDP in the nineteenth century to 50 percent in the first decade of the twenty-first century. So if—in Marx's day—an analysis of accumulation limited to consideration of Departments I and II made sense, this is no longer the case. The enrichment of Marxist thought by Baran, Sweezy, and Harry Magdoff (long-time editor with Sweezy of *Monthly Review*) through their taking account of Department III (and the linked concept of surplus, defined as we have recalled it) is for that reason decisive. I find it deplorable that this is still doubted by a majority of the analysts of contemporary Marxism!

Once again, not everything in this surplus is to be condemned as useless or parasitical. Far from it! On the contrary, growth in a large fraction of the expenditures linked to Department III is worthy of support. For a more advanced stage in the unfolding of human civilization, spending on such activities as education, health care, social security, and retirement—or even other socializing "services" linked to democratic forms of structuring alternatives to structuring by the market, such as public transport, housing, and others—would be summoned to take on even more importance. In contrast, some constitutive elements of Department III—like the "selling costs" that grew so fabulously during the twentieth century—are evidently of a parasitic nature and were viewed early on as such by some economists, like Joan Robinson, who were minimized or disparaged by their profession. Some public (weapons) and some private (security guards, legal departments) expenditures likewise are parasitic. A fraction of Department III, to be sure, is (or should we say was?) made up of spending that benefits workers and complements their wages (health care and unemployment insurance, pensions). Just the same, these benefits, won by the working classes through intense struggle, have been called into question during the past three decades, some have been cut back severely, others have shifted from provision by a public authority based

on the principle of social solidarity to private management sup-
posedly "freely bargained for" on the basis of "individual rights."
This management technique, prevalent in the United States and
expanding in Europe, opens supplementary, and very lucrative,
areas for the investment of surplus.

The fact remains that in capitalism all these usages of the
GDP—whether "useful" or not—fulfill the same function: to
allow accumulation to continue despite the growing insuffi-
ciency of labor incomes. What is more, the permanent battle
over transferring many fundamental elements of Department III
from public to private management opens supplemental oppor-
tunities for capital to "make a profit" (and thereby increase the
volume of surplus!). Private medical care tells us that "If the sick
are to be treated it must above all be profitable"—to private cli-
nics, to laboratories, to pharmaceutical manufacturers, and to
the insurers! My analysis of Department III of surplus absorption stands within the spirit of the pioneering work of Baran and
Sweezy. The necessary conclusion is that a large proportion of
the activities managed on those terms are parasitic and inflate
the GDP, thus reducing drastically its significance as an indicator
of the real "wealth" of a society.

Counterposed to this is the current fashion of considering
the rapid growth of Department III as a sign of the transformation of capitalism, its passage from the "industrial age" into a new
stage, the "knowledge economy." Capital's unending pursuit of
realization would thus regain its legitimacy. The expression
"knowledge capitalism" is itself an oxymoron. Tomorrow's economy, the socialist economy, would indeed be a "knowledge
economy": capitalism can never be such. To fantasize that the
development of the productive forces by itself is establishing—
within capitalism—tomorrow's economy, as the writings of
Antonio Negri and his students would have us believe, has only
a seeming validity. In reality, the realization of capital, necessarily based on the oppression of labor, wipes out the progressive

aspect of this development. This annihilation is at the core of the development of Department III, designed to absorb the surplus inseparable from monopoly capitalism.

We must therefore avoid confounding today's reality (capitalism) with a fantasy about the future (socialism). Socialism is not a more adequate form of capitalism, doing the same things but only better and with a fairer income distribution. Its governing paradigm—socialization of management over direct production of use values—thus comports exactly with a powerful development of some of the expenditures which currently, under capitalism, take part in its main function, surplus absorption.

ORDER OF MAGNITUDE OF THE IMPERIALIST RENT

In its globalized setup, capitalism is inseparable from imperialist exploitation of its dominated peripheries by its dominant centers. Under monopoly capitalism that exploitation takes the form of monopoly rents—in ordinary language, the superprofits of multinational corporations—that are themselves by and large imperialist rents.

In the propositions that I have put forward formulating the terms of a globalized law of value I stated the full importance of this rent.[6] Here I would like to give an idea of its quantitative scope in the capitalism of generalized monopolies and to link its effects to those associated with surplus absorption.

The order of magnitude of the quantifiable fraction of the imperialist rent, the result of the differential in the prices of labor powers of equal productivity, is obviously large. In order to give a sense of that order of magnitude, we hypothesize a division of the world's gross product in the ratio of two-thirds for the centers (20 percent of the world's population) and one-third for the peripheries (80 percent of the population). We assume an annual rate of growth of gross product of 4.5 percent for both centers

Year		Centers	Peripheries	World
1	Gross Product	66	33	100
	Wages	33	17	50
	Profits	33	16	50
45	Gross Product	132	68	200
	Wages	56	17	73
	Profits	56	17	73
	Department III	20	—	20
	Imperialist Rent	—	34	34

and peripheries, and a rate of growth of wages of 3.5 percent for the centers but total stagnation (zero growth) for peripheral wages. After fifteen years of development in this model we would arrive at the results summarized in the above table.

Of course, the volume of this imperialist rent, which seems to be on the order of half the Gross Domestic Product of the peripheries, or 17 percent of the world's Gross Product and 25 percent of the centers' GDPs, is partially hidden by exchange rates. It is a question here of a well-known reality that introduces uncertainty into international comparisons: Are GDP value comparisons to be made in terms of market exchange rates or according to exchange rates reflecting purchasing-power parities? Moreover, the rent is not transferred as a net benefit to the centers (United States, Europe, Japan). That the local ruling classes hold on to some of it is itself the condition for their agreement to "play the globalization game." But the fact remains that the material benefits drawn from this rent, accruing not only to the profit of capital ruling on a world scale but equally to the profit of the centers' opulent societies, are more than considerable.[7]

In addition to the quantifiable advantages linked to differential pricing of labor powers, there are others, non-quantifiable
but no less crucial, based on exclusive access to the planet's
material resources, on technological monopolies, and on control
over the globalized financial system.

The share of imperialist rent transferred from the peripheries
to the centers accentuates in its turn the global disequilibrium
pointed out by Baran and forms an additional factor, swelling the
surplus to be absorbed. The contrast to be observed during the
present phase of the crisis, between weak growth in the centers
and rapid growth in the developing countries of the periphery,
is to be understood only in terms of an overall analysis linking
analysis of how surplus is absorbed to analysis of the extraction
of imperialist rent.

CHAPTER NINE

Abstract Labor and The Wage-Scale

The concept of abstract labor, formulated by Marx, defines the common denominator allowing summation of different forms of simple (unskilled) and complex (skilled) labor. We are dealing with a concept central to the theory of value.

SIMPLE LABOR, COMPLEX LABOR, ABSTRACT LABOR

The unit of abstract labor, whether an hour or a year of abstract social labor, is a composite unit combining units of simple (unskilled) and complex (skilled) labor in some given proportion.

The concept of abstract labor is central to Marx's elaboration of the law of value, that is, to the determination of a commodity's value by the quantity of labor required to produce it and to the division of that value between wages and surplus value. The concepts of simple (unskilled) and complex (requiring training) labor are easily understood. But that of abstract labor is not immediately visible because a society's products do not stem from workers separated one from the other but from a collectivity, abstracted from which neither the least-skilled nor the most-skilled labor has any meaning: production requires their joint contribution.

We place the ensuing reflections in the context of a complete and closed capitalist system, which presents the three following characteristics: (1) the only form of commodity-producing labor is that which is supplied by wage workers who sell their labor power to capital; (2) the system by itself accounts for production of all consumer goods and producer goods in the proportions necessary to assure its simple or expanded reproduction; (3) there is no foreign trade.

Let us choose, from this society, a sample of one hundred workers distributed among the different categories of (differently skilled) workers in exactly similar proportions to their distribution in the overall society (whose labor force, for example, might number 30 million).

In the following simplified analysis we take account of only two categories of labor: (1) simple labor involves only 60 percent of the sample (sixty workers); (2) complex labor involves 40 percent of the sample (forty workers).

We assume that each year the workers in the sample provide the same annual number of labor hours, say, 8 hours per day and 220 days per year. So each of them provides, each year, a labor year amounting to 1,760 labor hours. Later we will calculate the quantity of labor years. So in each year a simple (unskilled) worker contributes one year of simple labor to the collective social labor, while a skilled worker provides a contribution to one year of complex labor. We abstract from the cost of training simple workers because this training is that which is provided to all citizens. Contrariwise, we take into consideration the cost of supplementary training for skilled workers. The latter, for example, would extend for ten years and for each of those years would cost, for each worker involved, the equivalent of two years of social labor to cover the cost of teachers, training equipment, and the student's living expenses.

Whereas the unskilled worker would work for thirty years, the skilled one would work for only twenty years, having devoted the first ten years to being trained. The cost of this training (twenty years of social labor) would be recovered over twenty years of this labor through the valorization of complex labor. In other words, the unit of complex labor (an hour or a year) would be worth two units of simple labor.

It follows that 60 percent of a composite unit of abstract labor would consist of the equivalent of one unit of simple labor, and 40 percent of the equivalent of one unit of complex labor (worth two units of simple labor). In other words, one unit of abstract labor provided by the labor collective is worth 1.4 units of simple labor.

I call attention to the following remarks:

1. The value of a commodity is to be measured according to the quantity of abstract labor required for its production because none of the workers works in isolation; he is nothing apart from the team in which he or she is a part. Production is collective and the productivity labor is that of the social labor collective, not that of team members taken separately one from the other.

2. I have put forth an extreme hypothesis in regard to the average cost of training for skilled workers. In the real world such training takes only a few weeks of apprenticeship for some, one or two years for others, and longer only for a few of the most highly skilled. A calculation comprising a dozen categories, allocated correctly according to their relative numbers, the time and costs of their training, and their labor time over the course of their entire lives would certainly reveal a value for an hour of abstract labor lower than 1.4 hours of simple labor. Abstract labor is not a "multiple" of simple labor; it is larger by a mere fraction.

3. I have accounted for the cost of training and its repayment without mention of any "discounting of the future," and so without assigning a "price" to time to take account of the fact that training time takes place before those costs are recuperated through the valorization of skilled labor. I have proceeded in this manner because the generations being trained, presently at work and in retreat, make up, all together, society as it exists at any given moment.

4. I have developed a line of argument based on the initial approximation. Training costs are to be measured in years of abstract labor (collective social labor), not in years of simple labor. One might develop a second corrective approximation. Or better yet, formulate a mathematical model that would introduce into the formulation of the interdependence of magnitudes the conversion of simple labor into abstract labor. Its results would not much differ qualitatively from those provided by my initial approximation.

5. I have not introduced into my argument the scale of real wages received by each category of workers, only the cost of their training, which is the sole "price" paid by the society to dispose of the labor force appropriate to its productions.

Production of Surplus Value, Consumption of Surplus Value

The value of the team's annual production and the measure of the extraction of a surplus value on this occasion are to be calculated in quantities of abstract labor.

Under hypothesis 1, and for our team of 100 workers, we assume that the real wage given to each skilled worker is double that of a simple worker, this relationship being that of the value of an hour of complex labor to that of an hour of simple labor. We have the above table.

	Contributions to the Formation of Value (Labor Years)			Contributions to the Formation of Surplus Value (Labor Years)	
	Hourly Labor	Abstract Labor		Wages	Surplus Value
Simple Workers	60	60	60	30	30
Complex Workers	40	40	80	40	40
Total	**100**	**100**	**140**	70	70

It is easy to recognize that the wage for a skilled worker is double that for an unskilled worker, as the former contributes twice as much to the value of the product as does the latter. Both equally contribute to the extraction of surplus value, in the same proportion. The rate of surplus value here is 100 percent. For an hour of labor provided by a simple worker, he receives a wage allowing him to buy consumption goods whose value is equal to one half hour of abstract labor. Each labor hour provided by a skilled worker is worth twice as much and likewise his wage is twice as large, allowing him to buy consumption goods whose value is equal to one hour of abstract labor.

We now take a wage scale different from that which would imply a equality between the wage and the contribution to the formation of value. In this second hypothesis the wage retained by a skilled worker is four times (rather than double) that of a simple worker.

We would then have the table below (see page 232). Under this hypothesis we recognize that only unskilled workers contribute to the formation of surplus value; the skilled workers "devour" the surplus value to whose formation they contribute.

It then is quite clear that if the wage scale for the various categories of skilled labor has a broad extent, going, say, from 1.5 to 2 times the subsistence minimum (the wage for unskilled labor)

	Contributions to the Formation of Value (Labor Years)			Contributions to the Formation of Surplus Value (Labor Years)	
	Hourly Labor	Abstract Labor		Wages	Surplus Value
Simple Workers	60	60	60	30	30
Complex Workers	40	40	80	80	0
Total	**100**	**100**	**140**	**110**	**30**

for many, three to four times as much for some, and much more for a tiny (extra-skilled) minority, we would recognize that if the majority of workers contribute to the formation of surplus value, although in different proportions (and this gives its full meaning to the term "super-exploited" for the majority—two-thirds—of the workers), there exists a category of the supposed "extra-skilled" (who may sometimes actually be so) who consume more surplus value than what they contribute to its formation.

SOME CONCLUDING REFLECTIONS

Marx's criticism of the classic bourgeois political economy of Smith and Ricardo concluded by a necessary shifting from analysis centered on "the market" (waves visible on the surface of the sea) to one centered on the depths of production where value and the extraction of surplus value are determined. Without this shifting of analysis from the superficial to the essential, from the apparent to the concealed, no radical critique of capitalism is possible.

In Marx's analysis there exists only one "productivity," that of social labor defined by "the quantities" of abstract labor contained in the commodity produced by a collective of workers.

There is improvement in the productivity of social labor when to produce a unit with a defined use value society can devote a lesser quantity of total abstract labor (direct and indirect). This improvement is produced by progress in the technologies put to work on the basis of society's scientific knowledge. One can compare the productivities of social labor in two production units making the same use values; contrariwise it is meaningless to compare the productivities of social labor in two branches of production making different use values. Thus to compare the general productivity of social labor in two successive epochs of capitalist development (or, more broadly, historical epochs), like productivity comparisons between two systems (for example, two countries), involves reasoning by analogy. The measure of this general productivity is obtained by calculating the weighted average of productivity progress in the different branches producing analogous use values. This is an approximate calculation, the number of use values needing to be considered far exceeding that available for consideration, and the weighting itself being partially dependent on the evolution of productivity in each of the branches under consideration.

The law of value formulated by Marx, based on the concept of abstract labor, expresses the rationality of the social utility (the utility for society) of a defined use value. This rationality transcends that which governs the reproduction of a particular mode of production (in this case, the capitalist mode of production). Under capitalism rationality demands the accumulation of capital, itself based on the extraction of surplus value. The price system frames the operation of this rationality. Economic decisions in this framework of given prices and incomes—themselves defined by the proportion in which value, termed value-added, is shared between wages and profits—will be different from those that might be made on the basis of the law of value that would define, in the socialism to come, the mode of social governance over economic decision making.

Bourgeois economic theory attempts to prove that the mode of decision making in the framework of its system of prices and incomes produces a rational allocation of labor and capital resources synonymous with an optimum pattern of output. But it can reach that goal only through cascading tautological arguments. To do so it artificially slices productivity into "components" attributed to "factors of production."

Although this pattern of slices has no scientific value and rests only on tautological argument, it is "useful" because it is the only way to legitimize capital's profits. The operative method of this bourgeois economics to determine "the wage" by the marginal productivity of "the last employee hired" stems from the same tautology and breaks up the unity of the collective, the sole creator of value. Moreover, contrary to the unproven affirmations of conventional economics, employers do not make decisions by using such "marginal calculation."

The wage scale under real capitalism is not determined by the cost of training skilled workers. It is broadly larger and has no other explanation except through considering the history of concrete social formations and class struggles. Its attempted legitimization through the "marginal productivities" of the contributions of different categories of workers is tautological.

The fundamental inequality in capitalism's characteristic distribution of income rests primarily on the contrast opposing the power of capital owners to the submission of labor power sellers. The wage scale comes as an addition to that. But the latter has by now acquired a new dimension. The contemporary capitalist system of generalized monopolies is based on an extreme centralization of control over capital, accompanied by a generalization of wage labor. In these conditions a large fraction of profit is disguised in the form of the "wages" (or quasi-wages) of the higher layers of the "middle classes" whose activities are those of the servants of capital. The separation among the formation of value, the extraction of surplus value, and its distribution has become wider.

References and Complementary Readings

This text makes up, with two articles published in *Monthly Review:* "Surplus in Monopoly Capital," *Monthly Review* 64/3 (July–August 2012); and "Abstract Labor," forthcoming), a trilogy that I hope will be read as a totality. The theses put forward in this abbreviated text were occasion for argued elaborations in the following of my works:

1. *The Law of Worldwide Value* (New York: Monthly Review Press, 2010)

- The unavoidable detour by way of value, transformation, divergence between profit rates expressed in prices and in values, the failure of equilibrium theories (Walras and Sraffa), price structure, and income distribution, are inseparable in the capitalist law of value (pp. 30–44).

- Chapter on rent: economic law or historical materialism? (pp. 77–81).

- Chapter on interest: State and money cannot be dissociated (pp. 64–70).

2. *Unequal Development* (New York: Monthly Review Press, 1976)

- Chapter on money and credit: the active role of credit in accumulation (critique of Rosa Luxemburg) (pp. 84–88).

- Chapter on money and credit: from the gold standard to floating exchange rates; national policies of regulating accumulation through credit (pp. 88–92).

3. *From Capitalism to Civilization* (Delhi: Tulika Books, 2010)

• The concept of the productivity of social labor; critique of the conventional theory of the productivity of factors of production (pp. 57–67).

The text barely sketches out the major question of globalization and the transformation of value into globalized value, a question constituting the prime object of many of my writings, the most recent formulation, *The Law of Worldwide Value*. Also to be considered: John Smith, "Imperialism and the Law of Value" (Ph.D. diss., University of Sheffield, UK, 2010). Our two studies, carried out unknown to each other, yielded similar conclusions about the origin of the contemporary imperialist rent. He likewise merely sketches two major subjects, financialization and ecology, for which I refer the reader to the following writings of John Bellamy Foster: *The Ecological Revolution* (New York: Monthly Review Press, 2009); and, with Fred Magdoff, *The Great Financial Crisis* (New York: Monthly Review Press, 2009).

Also see Samir Amin, "Capitalism and the Ecological Footprint," *Monthly Review* 61/6 (November 2009); and "Unequal Access to the Planet's Resources" and "The Extractive Rent" in *The Law of Worldwide Value*, pp. 95–100.

Concerning the nature of Marx's project, I refer the reader to Michael Löwy's excellent *Les aventures de Karl Marx contre le baron de Munchhausen* (Paris: Syllepse, 2012).

Concerning my rapid allusions to Marx's anthropology, see Yvon Quiniou, *L'homme selon Marx* (Paris: Kimé, 2011); and Anton Pannekoek and Patrick Tort, *Darwinisme et Marxisme* (Paris: Arkhé, 2011).

Concerning the subject of the power of capital, see Jonathan Nitzan and Shimshon Bichler, *Capital as Power: A Study of Order and Creorder* (New York: Routledge, 2009).

On the natural complement to this trilogy about the vision of long-run capitalism, see these works of mine:

- *Ending the Crisis of Capitalism or Ending Capitalism?* (Oxford: Pambazuka Books, 2011), esp. "Capitalism, a Parenthesis in History," pp. 56–59.
- *Unequal Development* (New York: Monthly Review Press, 1976), esp. "The Theory of the Balance of Payments," pp. 104–32. In this book, see my critiques of economic theories on international trade, of capital flows, and of fluctuations in the balance of payments. International political economy, which has certainly made a great contribution to correcting conventional economic theory, remains nevertheless limited by the positivist leaning of its methodology.
- Samir Amin and André Gunder Frank, "Let's Not Wait for 1984," in Samir Amin and André Gunder Frank, *Reflections on the World Economic Crisis* (New York: Monthly Review Press, 1978).
- "Market Economy or Oligopoly Capital?" *Monthly Review* 59/11 (April 2008).
- "Historical Capitalism in Decline," *Monthly Review* 62/2 (June 2011).
- *Beyond US Hegemony* (London: Zed, 2006), esp. "The New Imperialism of the Triad," chap. 1.
- *Obsolescent Capitalism* (London: Zed, 2003), esp. "The Political Economy of the 20th Century," pp. 7–17, and "The New Triad Imperialism," pp. 57–72.
- *Global History: A View from the South* (Oxford: Pambazuka Books, 2011), esp. "The Challenge of Globalization," pp. 67ff.

See also Isaac Johsua, *La crise de 1929 et l'émergence américaine* (Paris: PUF, 1999). Johsua calls attention to the new character of this crisis, which functions in an almost entirely waged society.

The analysis of the ongoing implosion of the globalized system of generalized monopolies and the discussion about the conditions for a socialist alternative do not make up the subject of this book, but see *The Implosion of Contemporary Capitalism* (New York: Monthy Review Press, 2013).

In this essay, I have not referred to the innumerable writings of Marxists who read Marx differently than I do. But I refer the reader to the writings of Suzanne de Brunhoff about Marx's monetary theory, according to which demand for money creates its supply. See S. de Brunhoff, *L'Offre de monnaie* (Paris: PUF, 1971). I believe that I have provided an indispensable complement to those writings by proving that the demand for money can be computed. I likewise refer the reader to the book by Nitzan and Bichler cited above. The latter part illustrates perfectly my thesis on "abstract" contemporary capitalism and its financialization. On the other hand, the preceding discussions in this book seem to me to stem from a positive reading that ignores the nature of Marx's project.

Notes

1. S. Amin and A. G. Frank, "Let's Not Wait for 1984," in *Reflections on the World Economic Crisis*, ed. S. Amin and A. G. Frank (New York: Monthly Review Press, 1978).

2. Samir Amin, *Empire of Chaos* (New York: Monthly Review Press, 1992).

3. Samir Amin, *The Implosion of Contemporary Capitalism* (New York: Monthly Review Press, 2013).

4. Samir Amin, *Unequal Development: An Essay on the Social Formations of Peripheral Capitalism* (New York: Monthly Review Press, 1976).

5. In this numerical example we assume that prices are proportional to labor values; that is, the organic composition of capital is the same throughout the economy and rates of exploitation (wages divided by profits) are also equal. If markets were competitive, then, as per standard neoclassical economic theory, wages would rise by the same percentage as the rise in labor productivity. In this example, wages would rise by 4.5 percent, the same as the increase we assume in productivity. However, under monopoly capital conditions, wages rise by less than productivity (abstracting from labor struggle that might force wages up). This means that over time the gap between the total output of a society and wages gets larger and larger. This is represented by the surplus in the last column of the example.

This surplus has to be absorbed somewhere in the economy to avoid stagnation.

6.   Samir Amin, *The Law of Worldwide Value* (New York: Monthly Review Press, 2010).

7.   In this numerical example, we extend the analysis of the surplus to the global economy. Here monopoly capital is able to move around the globe and use its economic and political power to pay workers in the periphery of global capitalism a wage considerably below that in the centers, even though their productivities are the same. For clarity of exposition, we assume that wages in the peripheral countries do not increase at all. This results in an enormous growth of surplus in the periphery, much of which is siphoned off as imperial rent and ends up in the centers via multinational corporations. The super-profits (based upon superexploitation of the wage labor) then have to be absorbed, making the stagnation tendency analyzed by Baran and Sweezy potentially more difficult to overcome.

Index

on contradictions in capitalism,
158; on crises in capitalism,
47; on Department III, 221; on
financialization, 65; on oligopolies, 28; on surplus, 162, 191,
217–18; on surplus absorption,
192; on third department in
capitalism, 49

taxation, 220
Taylorism, 47
technological change, 146
technology, 52
tertiary activities, 220
Third International (Cominform),
121
Third World, 121
Thompson, E. P., 132
time, 201–2; Marx on, 203–4
training of labor, cost of, 228–30
transformation problem, 183–84
transformed value, law of, 213
Trotsky, Leon, 159
true prices, 99
Tugan-Baranovsky, Mikhail, 23,
25

United States, 121; monopoly
capitalism in, 191
unproductive labor, 204
unskilled (simple) labor, 185,
227–30
use-value, 101, 173; measurement
of, 102–3

utopian socialism, 208

value: globalized value, 83–85,
210–12; in political economy,
132; price distinguished from,
31; social value, 173–74,
212–16; Sraffa on, 34–43;
transformation of, 12–13;
transformed into prices, 155–
56; wealth distinguished from,
207–8. *See also* law of value
Vietnam, 124

Wackernagel, Marthis, 100, 102
wages, 48; abstract labor and,
185–86, 227–33; growth in,
148; hypothesis of unchanging
real wages, 23–28; Sraffa on,
36–37, 40–43
Walras, Léon, 70, 156
Wang, Comrade, 123
weak sustainability, 103–4
wealth, 85; power tied to, 209;
value distinguished from,
207–8
women, 206
working class, 215
World Trade Organization
(WTO), 110

Zarembka, Paul, 159
Zhdanov, Andrei, 121–22
Zhou Enlai, 122–23